Military Aspects Of Ireland's Arms Crisis Of 1969-70

by

Angela Clifford

Arms Crisis Series No. 2
A Belfast Magazine No. 29

A Belfast Magazine

Arms Crisis Series

No. 1: ***August 1969, Ireland's Only Appeal To The United Nations***
a cautionary tale of humiliation and moral collapse
(A Belfast Magazine, No. 26)

Military Aspects Of Ireland's Arms Crisis Of 1969-70
by
Angela Clifford

is published by the
A Belfast Magazine

September 2006
ISBN 1 874157 16 2

Orders to:
athol-st@atholbooks.org
or
PO Box 339
Belfast, BT12 4GQ

Contents

Illustrations

Foreword To The Series

The 'Arms Trials' of September and October 1970 was a watershed in the political history of the Irish State.

A senior Cabinet Minister, Charles Haughey; a high-ranking Military Intelligence Officer, Captain James Kelly; a representative of the Catholic community in Northern Ireland, John Kelly; and Albert Luykx, a Belgian-born businessman, naturalised Irish, were charged with conspiracy to import arms illegally (for shipment to Northern Ireland). The charges against a second Cabinet Minister, Neal Blaney, were thrown out by the District Court. A trial was held in September 1970, but had to be abandoned when the Judge refused to continue it. A second trial was held in October. It ran its full course and resulted in Not Guilty verdicts.

Evidence at the trial hinged on the conduct of Captain Kelly. It was demonstrated, by the evidence of his military superior, Colonel Hefferon, that, in organising the purchase and importation of arms, he had acted under legitimate authority. Once that was demonstrated, any verdict other than 'Not Guilty' would have been a perverse verdict.

Captain Kelly acted on the instructions of Colonel Hefferon and was responsible to him. He also received direct instructions from Cabinet Ministers. If what he did was unauthorised by legitimate authority, and was therefore an illegal conspiracy, the illegality did not lie with him. He acted on the authority of his superiors, and his Colonel stated on oath that he had done so. It was not his business as a Captain to question the authority of his Colonel or of Cabinet Ministers.

If, after the evidence given by Colonel Hefferon regarding Captain Kelly, the political authorities still maintained that there had been an illegal conspiracy to import arms—and they did maintain it—then it was their business to bring a prosecution at the level at which the conspiracy existed. And that meant either Colonel Hefferon or the Minister to whom he was responsible. But it was not suggested that Colonel Hefferon acted without legitimate authority in the orders he gave to Captain Kelly. No prosecution was brought against him. Nor was a prosecution brought against the Minister for Defence.

The chain of legitimate authority was Cabinet Minister, Colonel and Captain. The reasonable presumption in each case—and it was in fact an obligatory presumption—was that the superior had legitimate authority for the instruction which he issued. It was not for the Captain to question the authority of his Colonel, or for the Colonel to question the authority of the Minister placed over him by the civil power.

The State did not, at the Trial, question the authority of Colonel Hefferon to give the instructions which he did to Captain Kelly. But, even if it had done so, and if it had been alleged that Colonel Hefferon had acted without authority, that would not have implicated Captain Kelly in illegal conspiracy.

Since the State did not question Colonel Hefferon's authority to issue his instructions to the Captain in the months after August 1969, it tacitly accepted that James Kelly had acted legitimately under the authority of the civil power. And if it presumed that Colonel Hefferon would give evidence that Captain Kelly acted on official instructions, the prosecution of Captain Kelly appears as perverse and irrational.

The Irish Army (or Defence Force) had ever since the mid-1920s been an orderly institution, diligently obedient to the civil authority. It was not an autonomous body, accustomed to supervising the civil power, or questioning the authority of the Minister of the Government placed in command of it. Indeed, the structure of the Army was such that it had no integrated existence as a corporate body, and was inherently incapable of concerted action independently of the civil authority.

The Cabinet took a close interest in military affairs and the Minister for Defence and his Department had a closer executive involvement in detailed military decision-making than might be expected. That is how it could come about that an Army officer could receive instructions directly from Cabinet Ministers: the Minister for Finance (Charles Haughey) and the Minister for Defence (James Gibbons) and the Minister for Agriculture (Neil Blaney, who had extensive contacts in Northern Ireland)—all of whom were acting on the authority of the Cabinet.

Colonel Hefferon gave evidence at the Trials that Captain Kelly had reported directly to the Minister for Defence. Consequently, as the Minister had the legal authority to give orders to Army officers, as well as to arrange for importation of arms, the prosecution seems bizarre.

That is how it appeared to the jury, which brought in a unanimous Not Guilty verdict.

But that was not the end of the matter. In some ways it was only the beginning.

While the *prosecution* must appear perverse to anybody who goes into the detail of the matter, the State treated the *verdict* as perverse. The suggestion was that the jury, in the grip of strong nationalist passion inspired by events in Northern Ireland, brought in a verdict which conflicted with the evidence presented in Court. The leaders of Government and Opposition, aided and abetted by the media, conspired to treat Captain Kelly as Guilty, and to dismiss the court verdict as being of no account. Even 30 years later Dr. Garret FitzGerald insisted on expressing this view—and had to pay hefty libel damages for it—or the *Irish Times* had to pay them for him.

The case against the other defendants also collapsed in the light of the clear and undisputed evidence given by Col. Hefferon in the case of Captain Kelly.

The laying of charges for criminal conspiracy which could not be made good in Court, and the persistence of both Government and Opposition in maintaining those accusations administratively, despite the failure to carry them through judicially, had profound consequences both for the body politic within the Republic and for the course of events in Northern Ireland.

The series of adjectives which Charles Haughey himself applied to another event many years later might be applied with even greater force to the vagaries of his own position at this point: grotesque, unbelievable, bizarre, and unprecedented—GUBU for short. He was charged with criminal conspiracy against the State by the Taoiseach who was his party leader, Jack Lynch. (It is inconceivable that such a charge might have been brought against a senior Cabinet Minister in those circumstances without the authority of the Taoiseach.) Lynch did not accept the Not Guilty verdict of the Court as being in accordance with the facts of the matter. He could not have done so without calling his own conduct into question. He continued to act as if a conspiracy against the state had existed and Haughey had been part of it. But he did not act to remove the conspirator from the Parliamentary Party or Fianna Fail membership. Haughey returned to the Lynch team in 1975, as shadow Minister for Health, becoming the Minister two years later. And Haughey replaced Lynch as Party Leader and Taoiseach just nine years after the Arms Trials.

Haughey can hardly be regarded as a victim of an act of injustice by the State of which he became Prime Minister, but there can be no doubt that the affair blighted his capacity to serve the nation. The Fianna Fail Party was badly damaged by the affair, and fractured by feuding connected with it. The most serious split was after Desmond O'Malley, who was made Minister for Justice by Lynch at the critical moment in 1970 and played a part in the prosecutions, failed to gain the leadership of the party when Lynch retired. He could not settle down under the leadership of Haughey—to be seen to serve under a man who, if the prosecutions were soundly based, had got away with criminal conspiracy against the state before going on to become Taoiseach; or conversely, to admit having been associated with a malicious prosecution. Following a series of attempts to overthrow Haughey, he resigned from Fianna Fail and founded a rival party, the Progressive Democrats.

Albert Luykx, the fourth defendant in the Arms Conspiracy Trials, was a refugee from the Fleming/Walloon conflict in Belgium who had made a new life for himself and his family in Ireland. He was recklessly dragged into Court by the State. A naturalised Irishman, he was asked by his friend, Minister Blaney, to assist Captain Kelly with his language and business skills. His brief involvement in the service of the Irish State was to prove costly, both in terms of his reputation and his business. When Justice O'Keeffe aborted the first Arms Trial, he put the entire legal costs onto Mr. Luykx. And after he was cleared, with the other defendants, Mr. Lynch's administration acted vindictively against his business interests.

Neil Blaney, though not a defendant in the Arms Conspiracy Trials, was a brilliant politician who was effectively driven out of politics by Mr. Lynch. Dismissed as Minister for Agriculture in May 1970, he was initially charged with Conspiracy to import arms illegally, with the other four defendants. Curiously, no evidence was brought against him in the July District Court hearing and the charges were dismissed. Cleared by legal process, his politics have been consistently misrepresented and reputation blackened: his crime being excessive adherence to Fianna Fail policy. In this he was another victim of Taoiseach Lynch's *volte face.*

John Kelly, following his acquittal, became involved in a new development in the affairs of Northern Ireland. He had grounds for seeing his prosecution as a betrayal by the Dublin Government of a movement which it had encouraged from August 1969 to April 1970.

The SDLP was founded in the Summer of 1970. Its founders had been engaged, along with John Kelly and others, in negotiations with the Dublin Government in the Autumn of 1969 for the supply of arms for defensive purposes to representative organisations of the Catholic community along with Defence Committee leaders such as John Kelly. That united political development was aborted by the change of policy in Dublin, and particularly by the abrupt and shocking way the change was announced.

The covert arms imports, which were the subject of the Arms Trials, were intended for use by the Defence Associations of the Catholic community in the North. Those Defence Associations had been made effective in August 1969 with the help of British ex-servicemen—Catholics who had served in the British Forces, and who had no general hostility towards Britain, but were not prepared to sit idly by while their community was maltreated by the devolved regime. Also involved were republicans, most of whom—like John Kelly—had put aside the gun years before, and an array of religious, community and political leaders.

The possibility of forming a new constitutional party of the Catholic community, which was connected with the Defence Associations, was blown away by the Arms Trials.

A new Republican movement, which was not limited to the defensive purposes of the Defence Associations, was brought into being and given powerful impetus by the combined shocks of the pogroms of August 1969 and the Arms Trials of 1970. The movement known as the Provisional IRA blossomed as an independent force in the Summer of 1970 as a consequence of the basic change of front by the Dublin Government signified by the arrest of Haughey, Blaney, John Kelly, and Captain Kelly. The Defence Associations withered away. The SDLP was formed as a merely electoral body in a situation where the normal framework for electoral politics did not exist. Although many of its founders had been involved in negotiating for arms, it began to strike pacifist attitudes and its leader, Gerry Fitt, adopted the practice of issuing libel writs against publications that hinted at his attempt to procure arms.

The ineffectual SDLP, formed in place of the more robust body envisaged by the Dublin Government from August 1969 to Spring 1970, might be regarded as a victim of the traumatic change of policy signified by the Arms Trials.

But the one undisputed victim was Captain Kelly, the diligent Army officer who had served the State faithfully for twenty-one years and then was blackguarded by it until his death, because it was found expedient to change policy and find a scapegoat.

But, though victimised, James Kelly did not break under pressure. He defied the State which had betrayed him. He published an account of the affair despite Government intimidation of publishers and booksellers. And, in the end, he discovered documents demonstrating how the prosecution had tried to rig the case against him. At the time of his sudden death he was bringing a legal action against the state for false prosecution.

The State has no defence against his indictment of it other than the use of its power. It refuses to apologise for its action. One of the reasons it cannot do so is that the party founded by his prosecutor, Desmond O'Malley, is a long-term partner with Fianna Fail. For many years it held major legal offices of State in the person of Michael McDowell, first that of Attorney General and then the Department of Justice, which was O'Malley's Ministry in 1970. The rehabilitation of Kelly would mean the disgrace of O'Malley. PD President Michael McDowell is determined that the founder of his party will not be subjected to disgrace while he has the power to block it. That is what *Justice* has come to mean in the Republic. The monarchical principle that the King can do no wrong appears positively honourable by comparison.

But much more is at stake in the Captain Kelly affair than the honour of Desmond O'Malley and Jack Lynch. The prosecution signified a change of direction in the conduct of the state which led to the general unravelling of its national culture.

This is the second of a series of reviews of the situation in 1969-70 in the North and the Republic with the purpose of showing how the Lynch Government responded to the Northern crisis in the first instance in the spheres of foreign policy, propaganda, and military arrangements; how it arranged the fiasco of the Arms Trials; and how the consequences worked themselves out.

Angela Clifford
September 2006

Introduction

"...No political Irishman, and least of all Mr. Lynch, can afford not to declare himself a republican..." (Report by British Ambassador John Peck, 30.6.70, PRO FCO 33 1206).

This is the second publication in the 1969-70 Arms Crisis series. The first, a pamphlet (*August 1969: Ireland's Only Appeal To The United Nations*), dealt with Ireland's diplomatic efforts in August-September 1969 to ameliorate the lot of the Northern Catholic community after the outbreak of civil rights disorders. This book concentrates on military aspects of the same endeavour, an effort which started in mid-August 1969 and continued right up to April-May 1970.

The immediate cause of the Arms Crisis was the failure of Northern Ireland security forces to maintain law and order in Northern Ireland, instead becoming a factor in the disorder in August 1969. Since the beginning of 1969, popular Unionist resistance to civil rights agitation had become increasingly violent, coming to a head in the 'Siege of Derry' of 12th-14th August, during which the RUC tried—and failed—to put down by force the spirit of rebellion in the Bogside. The Derry violence sparked conflagrations in other areas of the North.

In 1969-70 every political tendency in the Irish State agreed that the ultimate solution to the problems of the Northern minority was to end the arbitrary and unjust division in 1920 of the historic kingdom of Ireland. In that sense all were republicans. None would have disagreed with the suggestion in Jack Lynch's dramatic television statement of 13th August 1969 that the Northern Ireland crisis would only be settled, first by the granting of civil rights to the minority, and then by the *"restoration of the historic unity of our country"*. Nor would any have found fault with his declaration that, *"Recognising that reunification of Ireland provided the only permanent solution of the problem"*, he would be requesting the British Government to enter into early negotiations to review the constitutional position of the Six Counties.

Taoiseach Lynch is nowadays described by many commentators as a 'moderate', meaning some kind of crypto-unionist. But that is to misunderstand his position. He was sincere when he called for the restoration of Irish unity—insofar as a career politician can be. Lynch had become Taoiseach because of a well-developed capacity to ride events (as opposed to directing them). In August 1969, and in succeeding months, it seemed that the national wave of sympathy with the plight of the Northern minority would sweep away the weakened Northern sub-State, and that Lynch would ride that wave. It seemed realistic to allow that Unionism might shatter under the pressure of Home Secretary Callaghan's reform programme, and that there would be further serious attacks on Catholic areas which would put the future of Northern Ireland into the constitutional melting-pot.

Given that context, the Irish Government adopted a policy of maintaining diplomatic pressure for change, whilst preparing for military intervention, should the occasion for it arise.

In the event, Jack Lynch came under British pressure to change course in April-May 1970. Calculating that Unionism was not going to shatter, he dissipated the Irish wave of empathy with Northern nationalists with a powerful psycho-drama of Ministerial dismissals, arrests and prosecutions—a drama which gripped the country and gave cover to his *coup* within the Government and inside Fianna Fail, 'the republican party'.

For the first time Lynch directed events, as opposed to riding them, albeit only when forced to do so by others. By a malign reversal of the truth, he spread the rumour that the dismissed Ministers had been plotting some kind of *coup* against legitimate government. The converse was true: in so far as there was a *coup*, it was the Taoiseach who abruptly reversed a Cabinet policy of being prepared for all eventualities in favour of one of reliance on British goodwill in bringing about reform in the North, and British favour in keeping Ireland informed of its intentions. In strict constitutional terms this was not a *coup*, but a *volte face*—which is quite in order for a Taoiseach to do (if he can), and is why the dismissed Ministers continued to take the Fianna Fail whip.

The Appeal To The UN

But, back in August 1969, it was because Britain refused to negotiate about the future of Northern Ireland that the world diplomatic offensive was launched, culminating in the appeal to the United Nations. And the message of the diplomats and of External Affairs Minister Dr. Patrick Hillery was consistent with the Taoiseach's television speech of 13th August: Immediate granting of full civil rights and prompt negotiations to restore Irish unity were required.

The diplomatic context of that speech and of the crisis Cabinet meetings of 13th August and afterwards was Irish exasperation at Britain's failure to avert what it believed could easily have been prevented. Far from seeking the destruction of Northern Ireland, the Irish Cabinet had first tried to engage with it, and then to press for the speedy reforms which might have stabilised it. Jack Lynch and his Cabinet had continued the Lemass/O'Neill policy of Ministerial *rapprochement* until it was made irrelevant by anti-civil rights disorder.

After Premier Terence O'Neill was overthrown in April 1969 by a bombing campaign instigated by Unionist politicians using the Ulster Volunteer Force (and blamed on the Irish Republican Army, though it hardly existed as a force at the time), the Irish Government became increasingly concerned about the turn of events in the North. During an earlier Derry crisis in April 1969 External Affairs Minister Frank Aiken was sent to the United Nations, not to request any particular action, but to report to Secretary-General U-Thant what was happening in Northern Ireland—a move regarded with disfavour by Britain.

That disorder continued to escalate as the year went on. On 1st August the Irish Cabinet sent Dr. Patrick Hillery, Aiken's successor, to London to give a private warning that the traditional Londonderry Apprentice Boys' March of 12th August presented a particular danger point and pleading for the parade to be banned, re-routed, or curbed. He told Foreign Secretary Michael Stewart that *"if the situation were to "spill over" into violence, as was feared... he (the Minister) would come under increasing pressure to act"* (*August 1969: Ireland's Only Appeal To The United Nations* p9). Stewart rebuffed Irish attempts to prevent a conflagration, saying *"you accept, of course, that responsibility for this area rests with the Stormont and London Governments, and not with your Government"*, and adding *"there is a limit to the extent to which we can discuss with outsiders—even our nearest neighbours—this internal matter"* (ibid). In an internal memorandum, Foreign Office officials later discounted the Irish suggestion that serious disorder in Derry would force them to *"act"*, with the suggestion that such action could amount to *"recourse to the United Nations, or further discussion with the United Kingdom Government"* (ibid p10).

After the warnings of the Irish Government were vindicated, the Cabinet again sent Dr. Hillery to London, where he was seen by two Junior Ministers on 15th August. His mission was to press for inter-Governmental negotiations as well as urgent and dramatic reforms, which would take the heat out of Catholic agitation.

There had been a radical, if informal, change in the constitution of Northern Ireland between the two visits:

The RUC was unable to prevail against the Bogside and the Stormont administration had to call in the British Army on 14th August. The price to Unionism of this deployment was a loss of control of security powers (which was intended to be temporary).

And there had also been a change in the South: it was not quite a constitutional change, but it was far-reaching nevertheless. The people had become engaged with the position of the minority in the North and was eager to assist it in any way possible.

At his meeting with the two Ministers, Dr. Hillery warned that, given Irish history, the British forces deployed in Northern Ireland could easily become part of the problem: *"These troops are a provocation. Our people do not accept that*

Northern Ireland is not a part of Ireland" (ibid p18) These warnings were simply dismissed on the grounds that Catholics were welcoming troops as a protection against the security forces of the Northern Ireland administration.

The Irish Minister proposed an alternative: a deployment of a United Nations force (which could include Irish troops), or a joint Irish/British deployment. Lord Chalfont rejected this suggestion: *"This we could not accept in any circumstances. We could not agree to the deployment of a U.N. force on United Kingdom territory. The maintenance of peace on U.K. territory is a matter for the U.K. Government*" (ibid p18).

Dr. Hillery was simply stone-walled in this second interview, Lord Stonham declaring *"Nothing dramatic can be done"*—meaning that change would have to be introduced in Northern Ireland at a pace acceptable to the majority.

It was in that context that the Irish Cabinet framed a two-pronged military policy. One element was to appeal to the United Nations for help; the other was to prepare for an active Northern military policy. Both were innovations. Ireland had attempted to obtain a solution of the Border question first by engagement with British Governments, and then by engaging with the Stormont administration. Now it was going to circumvent British intransigence over the governing arrangements in Northern Ireland with a direct appeal to the United Nations. And, secondly, ever since the 1920s, Irish Governments had pursued a pacifist military policy with regard to the North. The Irish Army had never done any military thinking about the North, and there were no permanent military posts, north of a line from Gormanstown to Mullingar and Galway. Now strong forces were deployed to the Border, though under a cover story of establishing field hospitals and refugee camps, and military preparations for possible interventions were set in hand.

But a decision to appeal to the United Nations had a lot of ramifications, as the Irish Cabinet was to find. What exactly were the issues to be brought to the UN: was it the civil and political discriminations to which the minority was subjected in the Six Counties, or was it to be the partition of the historic kingdom of Ireland? Which body of the United Nations should be appealed to? The Irish could go to the Security Council, the General Assembly or one of its sub-committees. And under which Chapter of the United Nations' Charter was an appeal to be made?

The Department of External Affairs submitted a memorandum to the Irish Cabinet called *Bringing The Situation In The North Of Ireland Before The UN* (16.8.1969). This advised against raising Partition as a breach of the right to self-determination, and instead to concentrate on a Threat to Peace or on the Violation of Human Rights inherent in the governing arrangements for Northern Ireland made by Britain, leaning towards the latter.

It also advised against an appeal to the Security Council in the first instance, keeping such a move in reserve. The first approach should be to the General Assembly, which was due to meet in late September.

What the Cabinet decided to do was to go straight to the Security Council. It thought that matters were too urgent to wait a month for an appeal to the General Assembly.

And, rather than deciding on one ground of complaint, Dr. Hillery went forward with a mish-mash of all three: injustice of Partition; threat to peace resulting from governing arrangements; and breach of human rights of the minority.

But this strategy allowed Britain to prevent the item from appearing first on the Security Council agenda and later on that of the General Assembly. It was a premier object of its diplomatic policy to prevent the international community from examining, or intervening in, the governing arrangements it had made for Northern Ireland.

Britain would not have been able to block Security Council consideration of Northern Ireland if the 'threat to international peace' had been actual, rather than theoretical, that is, if the Cabinet had sent Irish troops to assist Bogsiders during the Siege of Derry. Though it could have vetoed any resolution criticising the governing arrangements which had necessitated such a move, this was an embarrassment it was anxious to avoid.

Using its diplomatic muscle, Britain prevented inscription of the *Six Counties* on the Security Council agenda, but arranged a face-saving device for Ireland, which allowed Dr. Hillery to make a speech to the Security Council.

Undeterred by this defeat (which was dressed up as a victory), Dr. Hillery embarked on the complex process of getting an emergency motion onto the General Assembly agenda. Again Dr. Hillery failed to concentrate on one ground of complaint. He was still in a confident frame of mind. Shortly before a crucial committee meeting to prepare an Agenda for the General Assembly, he lunched with British Ambassador Gilchrist at Britain's Dublin Embassy on 11th September. As Sir Andrew reported to London, when asked what his object was in going to the UN, Hillery replied:

> "...there was only one great object in his mind, the establishment of a single Government for the Thirty-Two Counties of Ireland. He added as a corollary that he would hope to teach the British something of the underlying realities of the Irish situation.
>
> ...
>
> I asked if the Irish had considered the future o Anglo-Irish relations in the context of their policy of taking us to court in New York. His first reply was that I could hardly expect him in this day and age t shed tears for the British Empire..." (*August 1969: Ireland's Only Appeal To The United Nations*, p62).

On 17th September, Dr. Hillery made a brief presentation to the General Committee of the General Assembly, which was preparing an Agenda for the General Assembly, declaring that *"the request to put the item on the agenda had not been made lightly. The situation was too grave for that..."* (ibid p67).

Lord Caradon then applied some serious moral blackmail: Britain needed a period of calm in order to reform the North, adding *"I think I know the Foreign Minister of Ireland well enough to say that he does not wish to be the one to strike the spark that would produce the explosion"* (ibid p68).

Deeply struck by these words, Dr. Hillery, instead of pressing the Committee to a vote on inscription, accepted an adjournment. When the Committee reconvened, the matter had disappeared from the agenda: another defeat under face-saving camouflage. Lord Caradon had dared Dr. Hillery to challenge British policy on Northern Ireland, and the Irish Minister flinched.

Dr. Hillery's moral collapse was made explicit at a further event, held in Britain's Dublin Embassy, around 12th November 1969. Oliver Wright (the UK Government representative in Northern Ireland) reported as follows to the Foreign Office on a conversation with the Minister:

> "4. Hillery had clearly been very impressed, not to say shaken, by his experiences in New York. It was evident that he had been surprised at the respect in which Britain as a nation and the United Kingdom Delegation as a delegation were held at the United Nations. He spoke in the warmest tones of respect and admiration of Lord Caradon and had clearly been much impressed by the Delegation's performance over the Irish complaint. He kept on talking about "fly-weights versus heavy-weights". But he seemed quite without rancour or resentment at his defeat at our hands.
>
> 5. Indeed, Hillery's view, the distillation of his experience over the past three months, seemed to be that none of us—Westminster, Dublin or Belfast—had put a foot wrong. Recollected in tranquillity, he even found satisfaction in his interview with Lord Chalfont at the beginning of August : he said that he quite understood that Lord Chalfont was right to refuse to take a more forthcoming line than he did, since this would have made Westminster's relations with Belfast more difficult; he himself had to express his dissatisfaction with the interview, but that in itself was helpful in the context of southern Irish opinion. Indeed the impression he gave was that, after all, all was for the best in the best of all possible worlds. Everything had happened as it had to happen and the main thing was that we had all come out of the ordeal pretty well intact : the Irish Government had been able to control their own public opinion; the Westminster Government had been able to get their programme of reforms launched and the Northern Ireland Government had survived as the instrument of those reforms. What more could anyone want?
>
> 6. Looking to the future, Hillery reinforced the impression which McCann had given me about the Irish Government's present policy on the unity of Ireland. This policy is clearly conducted at two distinct levels. The public policy is what one might call idealistic and incantatory and has to look forward, some

time round the Greek Kalends, to the unity of Ireland. The private policy is, however, more realistic and less ambitious : not only does it not envisage the possibility of a united Ireland for as far ahead as it is useful to look, but it is really not at all certain whether it actually wants it. That being so, I am sure the Irish Government will be satisfied with very modest conversations on the subject with us" (ibid, p88; Hugh McCann was the Secretary at the Department of External Affairs).

In a letter to London about this incident, Sir Andrew Gilchrist commented: *"Even in those [sic] days one achieves an occasional smirk of professional satisfaction"* (ibid, p87).

A couple of weeks later Dr. Hillery produced a Memorandum for the Irish Cabinet (*Policy In Relation To Northern Ireland)*, a section of which suggested that Irish unity could be accelerated if changes were made in the educational system: *"In teaching history in schools emphasis should be given to the positive aspects rather than the aspects which tend to be divisive"* (ibid p89).

The implication here is that teaching young people an inaccurate version of how and why Ireland had been conquered, misgoverned, and partitioned could reconcile the Northern Protestants to Irish unity. This view shows it was Dr. Hillery who did not *"understand the underlying realities of the situation"*, rather than Ambassador Gilchrist or the British Government.

Hillery was to initiate this changed approach to the teaching of history when, after initiating the Arms Crisis, Lynch put him in charge of a Sub-Committee charged with implementing some of the ideas in his Memo. Official promotion of revisionism is sometimes attributed to a desire to undermine public support for the Provisional War in the North. In fact, Hillery's memorandum shows that the official support for revising the teaching of history predated that campaign.

Did the Irish Cabinet really think that it would achieve anything with an appeal to the United Nations?

The one thing which might have brought results at the UN was an incursion into Northern Ireland, to bring aid to the citizens of Derry. But that would have been to make events, rather than ride them.

Given that the Irish Government was not at that point ready to break 'international law' with a Border violation, what did it think it could achieve with the UN appeal?

The Cabinet understood very well that Britain could veto any concrete UN interference in Northern Ireland. And no doubt it shared widespread illusions about the nature of the UN. But Ireland had been a conscientious supporter of the UN ideal and had built up a stock of 'moral capital' by contributing troops to UN peace missions in Cyprus and the Congo. The least it might have hoped for was some moral support in the shape of a meaningless UN resolution, or fact-finding mission. Dr. Hillery failed to gain even that. Thereafter Britain retained the diplomatic initiative in its dealings with the Republic.

The Military Response

As a result of document releases it is now possible to fit Captain Kelly's 1970 arms mission to the Continent into the context of the general military strategy of the Irish Government. State Papers explicitly record that Defence Minister Gibbons told Army Chief of Staff Mac Eoin in February 1970:

> "The Taoiseach and other Ministers have met delegations from the North. At these meetings urgent demands were made for respirators, weapons and ammunition the provision of which the Government agreed" (Document 16).

In the first instance, Army surplus weapons were set aside for possible distribution. Captain Kelly's mission was to facilitate the import of untraceable weapons which had been ordered by the Northern Defence Committees, and paid for from a Fund made up of public donations and Government money.

There is not much point in giving guns to civilians who do not know how to use them. That is why the Irish Government also provided military training of a general nature, first to a group at an Army camp and then by allowing individual enrolment in the defence forces.

State Papers also reveal that helping to arm the Defence Committees formed just one leg of the new military strategy adopted after August 1969. The Defence Forces were also ordered to prepare for interventions in Northern Ireland. But the Government found that decades of neglect had left them ill-suited to the new offensive strategy. Documents show extra resources were channelled to the military, and special training started. Above all, the Army started to think about the North in military terms.

Reproduced here is *Operation Armageddon*, the plan for a new war-game directed towards the North (Document 3). And a *Planning Board On Northern Ireland Operations* was established, three of whose reports are reproduced (Documents 8-10). Its remit was:

> "To report on the feasibility of the Defence Forces undertaking military combat or support operations, including the nature and implication of such operations" (Document 8).

It is significant that the Board complained that it had been given no *"clearly defined political objective"* within which to work. The reason for the lack of clarity was that the Government was keeping its options open about the context in which cross-Border incursions might be mounted.

Thus it was that the Planning Board considered four scenarios, the first of which was *"Attacks on the Catholic minority by Protestant extremists with which the Northern Ireland Security Forces cannot cope"* and the fourth was *"Conflict between Protestant extremists and Northern Ireland security forces not directly involving the minority".* These options involved assisting the authorities in Northern Ireland to maintain order, in the event of some kind of Unionist rebellion—which was Jack Lynch's dream scenario.

In the event, however, British Governments preferred to face down the minority rather than the majority. The initial object of British policy was to make cosmetic changes in Northern Ireland administrative arrangements, leaving the essential structure of permanent Unionist rule unchanged. Home Secretary James Callaghan knew very well that root and branch change was desirable in the North, and even drew up a constitutional scheme (a matter which will be returned to later in the series), but thought better of making fundamental change.

It was the Provisional war, which took off after Jack Lynch changed Government policy towards the North, that forced British Governments to address the impossible governing arrangements established in 1920.

Significantly, the third scenario for Irish military involvement in the North, which was addressed by the Planning Board On Northern Ireland Operations, was *"Conflict between Republican-Nationalist elements (possibly supported by illegal elements from South of the Border and the Northern Ireland Security Forces".* What the nature of such conflict might be is not specified by the Board.

The Planning Board concluded that there were serious obstacles to the Irish Army conducting successful overt operations across the Border on any large scale, but that there was scope for small interventions by specially trained forces and for covert assistance to the minority. Provision of arms and training are specifically mentioned as relatively easy for the defence forces to supply. As far as I have been able to tell, many of its suggestions were implemented. Amongst recommendations were—

> "23. The Board recommends that:
>
> a. a command structure be established to plan, organise, direct, coordinate and control operations in Northern Ireland, and that the structure be the subject of a separate study.
> b. a minimum of one infantry battalion in each Command area be brought up to full establishment strength as soon as possible and organised trained and equipped to operate in company groups, and that the Planning Staff, P&O be required to prepare a suitable battalion organisation to meet these requirements.
> c. The three motor squadrons to be brought up to establishment strength.
> d. A Special Forces Unit, prepared for employment, primarily, on unconventional operations be organised, trained and equipped in CTC [Curragh Training Camp]; the organisation establishment

[sic] of this Unit to be the subject of a separate study.

e. because of the training deficiencies and requirements reflected in the body of this report, an intensive training programme be initiated without delay by S/Trn to provide for the tactical proficiency of the units referred to in b, c and d above.

f. officer training be oriented on operational situations in a Northern Ireland setting.

g. the desirability of supporting the minority in the North by training and by the supply of arms and equipment be considered, and if found to be acceptable, the development of plans for the implementation of these courses.

h. the intelligence in the North be intensified and directed towards the courses of action suggested.

j. with regard to procurement policies, priority be given to the purchase of APCs, air defence weapons and riot control and demolition equipment.

k. a motivation programme be initiated aimed at indoctrinating our own troops.

24. The Board considers it necessary to draw attention to the following:

a. the provision of troops on the scale visualised will require a study of the present administrative commitments, dispositions and multiplicity of units (including Border deployments) and may involve the suspension of certain units and the closing of some posts,

b. the commitments in connection with operations in Northern Ireland will mean a diminution in the forces available for security and this problem will have to be met by an acceptance of the risk involved or by the call-up on permanent service of FCA elements.

c. there is a requirement to suspend all extra-military employment of the Defence Forces" (Document 8; there is no point *23.i.*).

Perhaps the most important documents to appear in this book are the three recording the Government Directive to the Army of 6th February 1970 (Documents 15-17). These indicate that the work of the Planning Board On Northern Ireland Operations was deadly serious and not just abstract projection.

The Army was ordered to prepare to intervene to protect the lives and property of the Northern Ireland minority, which implies an element of area defence, as opposed to brief mercy missions. And in subsequent documents there is some information on how the Army made arrangements to put these orders into effect, though there are clearly other documents which have not been put in the public domain (as is confirmed in Document 30).

All this continued right up to April 1970. It was towards the end of that month that the Taoiseach decided to call a halt to the Arms Importation Scheme, after he was put under pressure by the Permanent Secretary at the Department of Justice, Peter Berry—who was certainly not acting entirely on his own initiative.

What is notable is that at what was probably his first private meeting with Chief of Staff Mac Eoin in June 1970—after he had set in motion the process of criminalising those involved in Arms Importation for the Northern Defence Committees—Taoiseach Lynch did not reverse the military policy of the preceding months, or pretend that the Army may have been misled about Government intentions regarding the defence of the minority. He confirmed the order that the Army should to be prepared for incursions across the Border (Documents 25 and 26).

Chapters One and Two contain thirty released documents with a commentary, while Chapter Three documents the urgent demands for weapons from Northern leaders, and reviews some of the forms of official military assistance provided to the Northern minority. A short Appendix contains some comments from a retired Army officer on Chapters One and Two of this book.

In general, history is best written from publicly-available sources, such as newspaper reports, and parliamentary records. But, in the case of the Arms Crisis, such sources are flawed.

And even short quotations from State Paper releases are inadequate in providing a convincing picture on an issue which is as politically sensitive as Irish policy towards the North in 1969-70.

Those who made false accusations against the defendants in the Arms Trial were not simply 'economical with the truth' (in the words of a British Cabinet Secretary): they mixed economical truths with misinformation and downright lies. That is why substantial reproduction of released contemporary secret documents is required, so that the present generation can see what is fact and what is fiction.

The releases confirm the obvious: those who were on the receiving end of the 'conspiracy' allegations had every interest in seeing the truth emerge, while those who criminalised those carrying out Government policy had a vested interest in suppressing the truth.

Behind the Arms Crisis saga there is another battle over hearts and minds, which is why a new generation of commentators have joined the protagonists of 1970 in the misinformation game.

That is why the 30 documents in this book are so important. They are history, unadorned, unbiassed, real. Anyone who goes to the trouble of reading them can decide what happened and who has been telling the truth in the decades since the Arms Crisis.

Angela Clifford
September 2006

Chapter One

Military Responses In 1969

On 13th August 1969, with mounting civil disorder in Northern Ireland, and in response to desperate pleas from mainstream Northern nationalist leaders, the Irish Government, after an emergency Cabinet meeting, deployed troops along the Border with Northern Ireland. The orders given to the Irish Army were twofold: public and private. The cover story for sending the troops to the Border was that they were on a humanitarian mission to establish Field Hospitals and Refugee Camps for the Northern Ireland minority. In fact the Army was moved to the Border so that it could intervene if Catholic areas were overwhelmed.

The Army was further instructed to investigate the feasibility of assisting the nationalist minority in the North in various ways up to and including direct intervention beyond the Border.

At this point in time no Army was deployed in Northern Ireland—British or otherwise. Stormont was hesitating over whether to call in British troops, as Home Secretary Callaghan had told Premier Chichester-Clark that Britain would assume security powers in such an eventuality. The existing position was that, under the *Government of Ireland Act 1920*, responsibility for law and order lay with the Northern Ireland Minister for Home Affairs, who had tenuous control of the paramilitary police forces.

With Irish troops massed on the Border for the first time ever, with the Royal Ulster Constabulary unable to restore order, and under outside pressure not to send its B-Special forces into Derry, the Northern Ireland Government was forced to call for British military help. British troops were deployed in Derry on the afternoon of 14th August and in Belfast on 16th August 1969.

The Irish Army was maintained in readiness to assist nationalists and to cross the Border even after British troops were deployed in Northern Ireland.

Any Irish humanitarian intervention beyond the Border had inherent in it the possibility of a resumption of military conflict between the British and Irish States over Partition—a conflict which had been broken off 47 years earlier, in the Summer of 1922.

In August 1969 the Irish Army started to look at the North in military terms for the first time in two generations. For virtually five decades it had not thought about the North at all. Now a *Planning Board On Northern Ireland Operations* was established. Three of the *Top Secret* documents it produced have come into the public domain and are reproduced here. In one of these, dated 27th September 1969, *offensive* operations were contemplated. Co-operation with irregular forces was considered. Consideration was also given to the employment of unorthodox military measures of the kind which Britain described a *"ungentlemanly warfare"* when resorting to them after defeat in regular battle in France in 1940.

While such operations would require a major Irish commitment, the Planning Board pointed out that there were two easier ways in which the Northern minority could be assisted: training of civilians and supply of weaponry. We know that both of these ways of assisting nationalists under attack were implemented.

This Report confirms that Captain Kelly and the other defendants in the Arms Trials were not acting unilaterally.

The Planning Board calculation was that undercover military help of this kind could be given without bringing British retaliation.

At the same time the Army was funded to increase its size and to purchase additional hardware. Quarter-master's reports, including the 'shopping list' of wants, have been released and are reproduced here. The contents may surprise readers by their scope.

The desirability of diversifying away from British suppliers was emphasised.

Finance Minister Haughey took the unusual step of raising a loan in Germany—going outside the Sterling area of which Ireland was effectively part—to provide for contingencies.

Minister for Defence Gibbons—a leading Prosecution witness in the Arms Trials—convened the Council for Defence on 13th October 1969 which considered matters related to the new active policy.

All this challenged the culture and physical dispositions of the Defence Forces. The Irish Army was the peace-time force of a neutral State. It would not be much of an exaggeration to say that it had not fired a shot in anger since the Treaty War. Even during the Second World War 'Emergency' it thought purely defensively.

Following the 'Mutiny of the Major Generals' (1924), a military structure was devised that would discourage military flair and political ambition in the Army. The policy was continued by successive Irish Governments. Apart from the 'Emergency' years, the Army was kept short of funds, below strength, and physically divided in separate commands to prevent a *coup d'etat*. No single officer exercised ultimate command. Authority was shared between the troika of Chief of Staff, Adjutant General and Quartermaster General. Each reported directly to the Minister for Defence, who was able to exercise direct military authority. He arranged for co-ordination, sometimes acting through the Council for Defence.

Within days of the Regular Army being deployed to the Border, the Army Reserve was called up. The cover story here was that these men were required for possible deployment in the North in conjunction with the British Army or under UN auspices. The reserves were retained for active duty long after it became clear that Britain would not tolerate outside intervention.

However, Irish Peace-Keeping Troops were not recalled from United Nations service in Cyprus.

On 6th February 1970, with regular deputations of Northern leaders still lobbying for physical help, the Cabinet directed the Army Troika to prepare to assist Northern nationalists with weapons and to be ready to make military incursions into Northern Ireland in the event of a crisis situation.

In June 1970, a month after Jack Lynch initiated legal proceedings against those he accused of illicitly importing arms to assist Northern nationalists, he met the Chief of Staff and instructed him to continue military readiness to intervene in Northern Ireland for humanitarian missions (see Chapter 2).

All during the period under discussion—from August 1969 to June 1970—the Lynch Government continued to publicly deny this active policy of assisting Northern nationalists, and Taoiseach Lynch made 'statesmanlike' speeches about his policy towards the North, that is, thoroughly equivocal and evasive speeches which asserted the Constitutional claim to sovereignty over the Six Counties, while at the time suggesting that nothing was being done to give effect to the claim.

The Government Files now in the public domain tell a different story. The following documents show the Irish Army considering plans to act with nationalists in Northern Ireland, schemes which took in every option—including open intervention across the border, covert operations in Northern Ireland, and cooperation with irregular forces.

Particular attention should be paid to the Army supplies for which funding is sought in the documents reproduced below. The scope and power of the ammunition listed shows that military engagements are envisaged well beyond protecting Camps along the Border or safeguarding refugees approaching such camps. Supposedly, just 250 troops were to be deployed. In fact, far more were sent North. And the ordnance which Army chiefs thought might be required would have allowed for several days' fighting.

The documents are cited at length because they show that preparations were being made for war—and even to breach 'International Law'.

1. The Documents, 1969

Document 1: Deployment To Border, 14 August

"

Rng P70, CCA [Planning & Operations Section, Army Headquarters], Geata Na Páirce.
14 Lúnasa, 1969

"OO [Operation Order] No. 8/69

<u>SIT</u> [Situation]

1. A state of civil disturbance exists in NORTHERN IRELAND, particularly in the area of DERRY CITY. The Government of Ireland has directed that a military force will be deployed in the EASTERN portion of County DONEGAL, with a view to rendering such assistance as may be desirable.

<u>MISSION</u>

2. As explained verbally by CF [Chief of Staff] to Officer Commanding DONEGAL area.

<u>EXECUTION</u>

3. <u>Gen</u> [General] <u>Outline</u>: The operation will take the form of
   a. the establishment and location of 14 Infantry Group in the general area LETTERKENNY/BALLYBOFEY,
   b. the establishment of field hospitals at ROCKHILL and DUNREE.

4. …

5. <u>Tps</u> [Troops]

   a. <u>Ceann O</u> [Eastern Command] will provide
      (1) One Inf Coy [Infantry Company, approximately 140 all ranks]…
      (2) One MO [Medical Officer], one Sgt AMC [Sergeant, Army Medical Corps] and four med orderlies.
      (3) One MO (ROCKHILL).
      (4) One Sgt and two Cpls MPC [Corporals, Military Police Corps].

   b. <u>Ceann D</u> [Southern Command] will provide
      (1) One Inf Coy…
      (2) Four Med Orderlies.
      (3) One Sgt and two Cpls, MPC.

   c. <u>Ceann I</u> [Western Command] will provide
      (1) One Inf Coy…
      (2) Gp HQ and HQ Coy - See Annx "b" [Group Headquarters and Headquarters Company].
      (3) Four med. orderlies.
      (4) One MO and four med NCOs (DUNREE).
      (5) One MO and four med NCOs (ROCKHILL).
      (6) One Sgt and two Cpls, MPC.

   d. CTC [Curragh Training Camp] will provide
      (1) One MO, one Sgt and four Cpls, AMC.…
      (2) One Sgt and two Cpls, MPC.
      (3) Five nurses, ANS (ROCKHILL).
      (4) One MO (DUNREE).

   e. <u>Command</u>
      (1) DONEGAL area - COL. M.J. BUCKLEY.
      (2) 14 Inf Gp [14th Infantry Group] - LT. COL. M.J. MURPHY.
      (3) Four Med/MPC [Medical/Military Police Corps] sections in DONEGAL area - COMDT. J. FAGAN.

6. <u>Tasks</u>

   a. <u>14 Inf Gp</u>: to be issued by OC [Officer Commanding] DONEGAL area.

   b. <u>Med/MP Sections</u>:
      (1) Set up standing patrols in the REPUBLIC OF IRELAND on main routes leading from DERRY into County DONEGAL.
      (2) Treat and evacuate casualties and refugees as required to fd hosps [field hospitals] at DUNREE and ROCKHILL.

7. Coord Instrs [Co-ordinating Instructions]

a. Assembly Area

...

b. LOCS

...

c. Timings

(1) Coys [Companies] will move to Assembly Area without delay but not later than 0100 hours[One a.m.] 14 Lúnasa, 1969.

...

ISSUED BY DIRECTION OF AN CEANN FÓIRNE

CORNAL S.C. Ó DONNABHÁIN
S P70

AUTH Lt. Col J. ADAMS
OF Rng P70

SECRET

[National Archive, Planning & Operations, File 1. No Annexes were in the file, as released to the public. I am indebted for help with military formations and abbreviations to a retired officer.]

Comments: The document is *"issued by direction of an Ceann Fóirne* [Chief of Staff] and signed by two other Army Headquarters staff: Col. S.C. Ó Donnabháin, Director of Planning and Operations; and Lt. Col. J. Adams of the Planning and Operations Section.

While the situation report states that the deployment is being made with *"a view to rendering such assistance as may be desirable"*, it is noteworthy that the *"Mission"* has not been put in writing.

The numbers and profile of troops deployed, as indicated in this document, do not indicate more than a humanitarian mission. There are three separate infantry companies, an extensive medical team and the other troops could be protecting the camps, or providing a screen for refugees who are crossing the Border.

It is from other sources that we know that possibly 1,000-1,500 troops were deployed to the Border in August 1969. And it is these numbers that are more in keeping with readiness to mount "incursions" into Northern Ireland, rather than with guarding the five Field Hospitals and the Refugee Camps that were established south of the Border.

It will be noticed that the forces for this operation are drawn from four different Command Areas.

Document 2: Plan To Enter Coleman's Island, Undated

[This project did not make much sense until I was informed that Coleman's Island was the part of the Republic which is practically surrounded by County Fermanagh. A "concession road" from Clones to Butlersbridge goes through it. "While Gardai could travel on this road by removing their caps, I believe it was felt that the army could not do the same. I remember talk that some army personnel had to travel across country in order to set up roadblocks there. I believe this activity was more in showing the flag in an area that was completely cut off" (a retired Commandant, 23.8.04).]

"

<u>MEMO</u>
<u>COLEMANS ISLAND</u>

1. <u>METHODS OF ENTRY</u>

a. <u>MILITARY.</u> RIVER CROSSING
heli [helicopter] landing.

b. <u>GARDAÍ</u> BY ROAD (CONCESSION RDS).

2. <u>SIZE OF PARTY.</u>

a. The size of party required in COLEMANS ISLAND depends on the task to be performed.

b. <u>TASK I.</u> <u>Showing of military presence.</u>
The showing of a military presence is important but its real effect can be manifested only when accompanied by Gardaí who have the legal power to search vehicles, houses and other property.

c. <u>TASK II.</u> <u>Rd Blocks</u>
If the task is to set up a road block or road blocks then the size of military may vary from 1 NCO 4 Ptes for one Rd Block to that figure multiplied by the No. of Rd Blocks required.

d. <u>TASK III.</u> <u>Search</u>
If the task is to search then the strength should NOT be less than 20 which would include an officer i/c [in charge].

3. <u>Surprise.</u>

a. When the method of entry is by river crossing it must be assumed because of distance to be travelled, equipt [equipment] to be used and, restricted entry route, that the element of surprise will not be on the side of the military force.

b. If Helicopter is used as method of entry then the element of surprise should be on the military side. However the fact that Gardaí may be required on the ground prior to the arrival of Helicopters may take away the military surprise element.

c. O/Night[Overnight] operations would I feel be advantageous to us but for such ops [operations] strength must be adequate.

4. <u>Likely results from military patrolling of COLEMANS ISLAND</u>.

a. By the presence of military patrols in the area subversive movement of Personnel and Equipt could be disrupted.

b. If such movement is taking place the capture of such equipment is conceivable.

c. Denial of perhaps a short term haven for subversives.

d. A strengthening of the will and opportunity for Gardaí to be more active in the area.

e. A showing to NORTHERN security forces that COLEMANS ISLAND which they may feel is a "NO GO" area to our forces in in fact NOT such."

[Undated and unsigned ; National Archive, P & O, File 1.]

Comments: Clearly Coleman's Island is important strategically. It provides an entry point into Northern Ireland from the south, but it could also be easily cut off from the rest of the country. One aspect of Army thinking at this time was defence of the Republic against incursions and counter-strikes from the North: a particular consideration was that Co. Donegal could easily be cut off.

Document 3: Exercise Armageddon, Undated

" SECRET

Ex [Exercise] ARMAGEDDON

Introduction

1. Ex ARMAGEDDON is a two-sided war game. It is an on-going exercise which will be utilised continually and repetitively, if necessary, in order to achieve the aims for which it is conducted.

Aim

2. The aim of Ex ARMAGEDDON is:—
To study, plan for and rehearse in detail the intervention of the Defence Forces in NORTHERN IRELAND in order to secure the safety of the minority population.

Analysis of the Aim

3. In achieving the aim of the exercise, it is visualised that there are several phases to be studied and planned. The starting point is clearly the report to be submitted by the Board currently studying the problem [i.e. the Planning Board For Northern Ireland Operations: see Documents 8,9, and 10]. On submission of the outline plan, preparations should be made to commence Ex ARMAGEDDON. It is visualised that there are several component aims to be achieved in the exercise as follows:—
   a. To test and assess operational plans.
   b. To carry out feasibility studies.
   c. To formulate detailed operational plans.
   d. To test formation and unit organisation.
   e. To exercise commanders and staffs in the conduct of operations.
   f. To rehearse operations.
   g. To determine the requirements for further recce, EEI [Essential Elements of Information] and the further development of operational plans.

SECRET.

Ex ARMAGEDDON

Introduction

1. Ex ARMAGEDDON is a two-sided war game. It is an on-going exercise which will be utilised continually and repetitively, if necessary, in order to achieve the aims for which it is conducted.

Aim

2. The aim of Ex ARMAGEDDON is :—

To study, plan for and rehearse in detail the intervention of the Defence Forces in NORTHERN IRELAND in order to secure the safety of the minority of population.

Analysis of the Aim

3. In achieving the aim of the exercise it is visualised that there are several phases to be studied and planned. The starting point is clearly the report to be submitted by the Board currently studying the problem. On submission of the ~~plan~~ outline plan, preparations should be made to commence Ex ARMAGEDDON. It is visualised that there are several component aims to be achieved in the exercise as follows:—

a. To test and assess operational plans.
b. To carry out feasability studies
c. To formulate detailed operational plans.
d. To test formation and unit organisation
e. To exercise commanders and staffs in the

Exercise Armageddon, first page

h. To analyse further requirements of equipment, and organisation necessary to accomplish the task.

Concept

4. It is clear from the analysis of the aim that Ex ARMAGEDDON is a continuing war game which will be played over and over again in order to clarify problems and produce solutions to problems.

5. It is essential that the war game be two-sided. In order to reduce the artificial nature of the "enemy" side, it is essential to have 'enemy' commanders complete with staffs who will actively oppose the intervention with the forces at their disposal. The "enemy" commanders should not be appointed "just for the exercise". It is visualised that 'enemy' commanders will have a detailed knowledge of the terrain, of their own forces, and of Irish Defence Forces so that they can plan realistically. Therefore, they will have to live as 'enemy' commanders. They should be of colonel rank and preferably, should be brigade commanders.

6. In order to make adequate preparations, it is thought that the preliminary exercise could NOT be held before the end of May at the earliest. However, after that it should be possible to hold the war-game more frequently, certainly it should be held at least four times each year.

OUTLINE ORGANISATION

7. Since this paper is an outline paper, it is NOT possible to give a detailed organisation for the exercise. There are four main groups in the war game:-

a.	Control Staff responsible for preparing the war-game and conducting the exercise.	Comdt, Mil Coll [Commandant, Military College] and Selected Staff of C & S [Command & Staff] School.
b.	Observer and Umpire Group - responsible for assessing the assessing the activities of the various forces and assessing if the aim has been achieved.	Directors and Selected Staff Officers Chief of Staff's Branch AG's [Adjutant General's] BRANCH [Army HQ] QMG's [Quarter Master General's] BRANCH [Army HQ].
c.	BLUE FORCES. i.e 'our' forces.	Comd [Command]: COL [Colonel] with a number of brigade comds (COLS) [Colonels].
d.	RED FORCES. i.e. 'enemy' forces	Comd: COL with two other COLS with staffs.

PREPARATION

8. A detailed directive would be prepared after a study had been carried out in Chief of Staff's Branch. The directive would fix responsibilities for the various phases of preparation for the exercise, appoint commanders, and detail the necessary arrangements for the exercise.

Security

9. Security Classification: Ex ARMAGEDDON will be classified 'SECRET' at all times.

10. Documents/Discussions

a. All documents relating to the exercise will be held by the Operations Section, Chief of Staff's Branch except when the exercise is being prepared or conducted, in which case, all documents will be held by the Commandant, Military College.

b. All copies of documents will be numbered and signed for by recipients.

c. The taking of notes from or the reproduction of documents in any form is forbidden.

d. Ex ARMAGEDDON will NOT by discussed by exercise planners, control staff observers or players outside the locations of the Military College or AHQ [Army HQ]. The war-game will NOT be discussed with any one NOT authorised to take part in the war game.

e. All papers used in the exercise will be collected and either destroyed or filed in Operations Section, AHQ.

f. Maps will NOT be referred to on exercise documents by name or map number. A code list of maps will be prepared and maps will be referred to as MAP A, MAP B etc.

g. Nomenclature:
(1) N Ireland will be called REDLAND.
(2) REPUBLIC OF IRELAND will be called BLUELAND.
An order of battle [list of units] will be prepared for REDLAND FORCES.

Communications.

11. During the war game, communications will be maintained by field telephone and by sealed, hand-delivered message. Radio will NOT be used.

Security Officer

12. A Security Officer will be appointed.

Personnel.

13. The Personnel taking part as players must hold the actual appointment of Commander or staff officer. 'Ad hoc' filling as appointments will NOT be permitted. All Personnel taking part in the exercise must be approved by the Chief of Staff.

14. Normally, the war game will be conducted in the Military College."

[National Archive, P & O, File 1, hand-written document; EEI, or Essential Elements Of Information are put as questions—for instance, What is the enemy strength?, How is the enemy equipped?, What is the enemy morale?.]

Comments: The exercise outlined above is clearly a means of secretly rehearsing the Irish Army for incursions into Northern Ireland. The document is not dated, but it probably dates from September-October 1969. Paragraph 3 mentions that the exercise would be based on the conclusions of the Planning Board On Northern Ireland Operations, which is *"currently studying the problem"*. We know that this Board produced an Interim Report on 27th September.

The reference to the Planning Board's deliberations lends a practical aspect to this scheme for a war game to rehearse Irish forces for Northern Ireland operations.

The author says the Army would not be ready for extensive manoeuvres as regards Northern Ireland for another 7-8 months. It was around May 1970 that Taoiseach Lynch moved against Cabinet colleagues and against Captain Kelly.

Ex Armageddon is not signed. It is handwritten for security reasons. It clearly envisages the Commandant of the Military College playing a central part in the operation. Certainly he is to prepare the war game for playing and be the 'Control'. The Commandant of the Military College at this period was Colonel Thomas L. O'Carroll (who became Chief of Staff in August 1971).

Other staff listed for participation include Training Officers at the Command & Staff School. At that time this School was headed by Colonel P.J. Delaney, who was appointed Colonel Hefferon's successor as Director of Military Intelligence in April 1970. (He was also the man who helped to marshal army resources to assist the prosecution prior and during the Arms Trials—particularly against Captain Kelly. He also tried to criminalise Captain Kelly behind the scenes during the Dail Public Accounts Committee hearings into the arms importation. In his statement for the Arms Trials he claimed to have been kept in ignorance of the Arms Importation operation and complained that Colonel Hefferon did not brief him about that venture. Whatever about that, *Ex Armageddon* shows that he was amongst a small circle of officers who were to prepare for Northern incursions. He was later promoted to be Chief of Staff over the heads of more senior officers, but died in office soon afterwards.)

Document 4: Supply Deficiencies, 19 August

[A letter to from Colonel MacDonnchadha/Donagh, Quartermaster General, to the Secretary of the Department of Defence, Seán Ó Cearnaigh, marked *Secret* on every page and dated 19th August 1969, indicates the supply deficiencies of Irish military forces—]

" *Sicréideach* [Secret]

Braine An tArd-Cheathrunaigh.
[Quarter Master General's Branch]
19 Lunasa 1969.

An Runai.

Supply Requirements - Na Forsai Cosanta [Defence Forces]

1. Since 18 Lun [August] 69 Na Forsai Cosanta

   a. has deployed approximately 1,500 troops in the field to set up and maintain Field Medical Hospitals and Refugee Camps,

   b. called up the First Line Reserve,

   c. cared for hundreds of refugees.

   This operation has indicated that deficiencies in our supply position exist and the following paragraphs describe our most urgent requirements of commodities most of which are already catered for in current estimates.

2. Communications Equipment

a. Priority requirements:

(i)Subhead p.1(1)(11) - VHF [Very High Frequency] Mobile Radio Telephone Equipment consisting of 3 Base Stations and 18 substations. Requisition No.10 of 1969/70 refers.

(ii) VHF Radio Telephone Equipment consisting of 9 fixed and 1 mobile station. References...

b. Very urgent requirements

(i)...20 HF [High Frequency] Manpack Transmitter/Receivers.

(ii) ...4 VHF Radio Telephone Equipments.

(iii) ...Line Equipment

(iv) VHF Radio Telephone Equipment consisting of 1 fixed and 4 mobile equipments - replacements for CTC [Curragh Training Camp] security equipment....

(v) Batteries and cells - present stocks of dry batteries, accumulator batteries and telephone cells and quantities on requisition are adequate for training purposes only. It is now urgently required that arrangements be made to have these items available on demand from supply sources.

3. Barrack Services

	On Order	Additional requirement
a. Blankets (all patterns)	6,400	15,000
b. Mattresses (do.)	1,720	3,750
c. Pillows (do.)	1,820	3,500
d. Pillow cases (do.)	7,700	10,000
e. Sheets (do.)	7,180	11,000
f. Tables	210	1,500
g. Dining hall chairs	870	To be calculated

4. Our troops in the field urgently need sleeping bags of which we have NONE. We require 5,000 sets.

5. Clothing and tentage

...

6. Cooking equipment:

...

7. Defensive Equipment

a. The procurement of the items provided for in current estimates is, now, a matter of great urgency.

b. Special mention must be made of our ammunition position. For the weapons available to the Defence Forces and on the basis of their employment the duration of fire at combat rates within present stocks will NOT exceed the following figures.

25 pr [pounder]	-	1	day
120 mm Mor [Mortar]	-	1	day
81 mm Mor	-	2	days

60 mm Mor	-	2	days
84 mm Atk [Anti-Tank] HEAT	-	1 1/2	days
84 mm Atk HE [High Explosive]	-	1	days
90 mm Atk HE	-	Nil	
FN [Fabrique National] Rifle	-	2	days
Submachine Guns	-	1 3/8	days
Light MGs [Machine Guns]	-	1	day
Vickers MGs	-	1	day
AA [Anti-Aircraft] Guns	-	1	day
Hand Grenades	-	Some hours (stock - 6,000: requirement is 250,000)	

It is evident, therefore, that with the possibility of our Forces being engaged in sustained operations the need for the establishment of rapid resupply sources is both urgent and vital. The diversification of our present supply sources and their location must be borne in mind.

c. This position also applies to our stocks of anti-riot grenades, 84mm Smoke and Illuminating ammunition Signalling Ctges [Cartridges], Energa Grenades, and Energa Ballistite which latter is in particularly short supply.

d. A figure of 10,000 modern respirators [gas masks] are required.

f. Medical and Military Police Equipment - the position is being reviewed."

[NA S 650; 'mm' is Millimetre; 'the *FN* is a Belgian rifle; information from retired Army officer and Conor Lynch, to both of whom I am indebted for comments on this chapter and help with Irish terms.]

Comments: The date on the letter is significant: the Army did not waste any time preparing its dispositions for possible offensive operations.

The first part of this letter is requesting authorisation to purchase normal supplies to provide for the refugees the Army is caring for. It is a different matter with the supplies listed under the heading, *Defensive Equipment.* Some of the equipment listed is anything but *defensive.*

The first item on the list, the 25 pounder ammunition, is for artillery pieces which, with mortars, are indirect weapons. Their trajectories are curves, steeper depending on proximity of target. Certain artillery pieces have much longer ranges than any mortar of any calibre. In World War I it was used in artillery barrages preparatory to infantry assaults. It is the type of weapon that was used by the British Army against the Irish rebels in 1916 and by the Free State against the anti-Treatyites in the Four Courts. The ordnance is heavy. Even though the guns may have been ancient, they were still potent.

The next three items on the list are mortar ammunition. These mortars are big guns: the 120 mm is a hefty weapon, which is on wheels.

The HEAT ammunition is defensive and is a grenade that is used against against armoured vehicles or tanks. It will penetrate metal and burn the interior. It can also be used against buildings The HE ammunition is offensive. Both are listed above.

A peculiarity which emerges is that the troops profiled in Document One above are infantry: no artillery companies are mentioned. But some of the ammunition on the Defensive Equipment list is for weapons that are fired by artillery units: the Twenty-Five Pounders and the 120 mm mortars. Clearly there were further deployments of Irish troops for which no documentation has been released into the public domain. The requisition of 5,000 sleeping bags for troops is of interest in this context.

Three different kinds of machine guns appear on the list above. These are infantry weapons. The Irish Army was equipped with Carl Gustavs, a modern Swedish weapon. There would also have been a number of Light Machine Guns, which could be carried by a soldier, along with one magazine and a bipod for the piece to be mounted on. These may have been Bren Guns. Another weapon held would have been the Vickers Machine Gun, a weapon used in a relatively fixed position. This was the standard British machine gun in the First World War.

The Anti-Aircraft Guns, for which there was only one day's ammunition in stock, would be defensive in nature.

Paragraph 7c mentions Energa Grenades. These are fired like a mortar and the Energa Ballistite is a form of blank which might be used to fire the grenades. This is a potent weapon which could be used against crowds of people or masses of troops.

The reader may be surprised to see that the Army considered 6,000 as an insufficient number of Hand Grenades for the purpose in hand, and was requesting funds to buy 250,000. After all, ostensibly such weaponry was only to protect Refugee Camps and Field Hospitals from a most unlikely attack!

The figure of 10,000 respirators raises the question of who these were for. It must be assumed that some, at least, of these were intended for civilian use in the North. The RUC used tear gas during the Siege of Derry: the first time it was used in the UK.

The radio equipment ordered would seem to allow for three command posts with six groups reporting to each.

Colonel MacDonnchadha/Donagh also suggests that thought be given to the location and sources of suppliers of Irish weaponry. In fact, the Irish Army started diversifying its weaponry on a large scale after the deployment in the United Nations' Congo operation in 1961. It acquired the Gustav to replace the Thompson. The Belgian FN rifle was got to replace the British Lee Enfield. Uniforms were obtained from Denmark.

In many ways the Irish Army was ahead of the British: it introduced semi-automatic rifles and automatic weapons earlier. It had a heavy fire-power philosophy, which envisaged close quarter combat.

This letter from the Quartermaster General to the Department of Defence makes clear that the Government instructions to the Army to prepare to render assistance to the Northern minority went beyond simple defence of hospitals and refugee camps within the State. The supplies requested are both pacific and military. The military weapons on the list are both defensive and offensive. It must be assumed that the Irish Army was not expecting an unprovoked attack, so the defensive weapons would be needed to protect against retaliation for its own actions North of the Border.

High explosive, anti-tank, mortar and machine-gun ammunition and Energa grenades were not going to be needed to defend Field Hospitals and Refugee Camps from low-level assaults, but they would be required for "intervention of the Defence Forces in NORTHERN IRELAND in order to secure the safety of the minority population" (Ex. Armageddon).

Document 5: Calculating Combat Supplies, 21 August

[Further *Secret* letter from Col. MacDonnchadha/Donagh, Quartermaster General, addressed to "Contracts Officer"—who presumably had queried how the combat requirements of ammunition had been calculated:]

" *Sicréideach*

Copy No. 1
Brainnse an tArd Cheathrunaigh.
21.8.69.

Contracts Officer.

Supply Requirement - Na Forsai Cosanta.

1. Yours of 21/8/69 refers.

2. Defensive Equipment The time estimates given in my letter of 19/8/69 are calculated from data commonly available to military staffs. Such data is arrived from War experience and is used in all armies for such logistical calculations. They relate stocks of ammunition to the numbers of available weapons in each class.

3 The diversification of our present supply source also applies to 25 pr ammunition and, since the main source is British, the General Staff is anxious to know of alternative markets.

4. I am anxious that immediate steps be taken to ascertain the available sources to meet our ammunition requirements, the possibility of supply from sources, and the time element re delivery."

[NA S 650.]

Comments: I did not find the letter from the Contracts Office to which Col. MacDonnchadha/Donagh has replied on the same day. It seems that a query had been raised as to the amounts by ordered by the Quarter Master.

The request to examine possible alternative suppliers for 25 pounder ammunition is significant.

Document 6: Military Stocks, 27 August

[This is the response to Col. MacDonnchadha's list of requirements. It is dated 27th August 1969 and addressed both to *Rúnaí Cúnta* [Assistant Secretary] and to the Secretary at the Department of Defence:]

"1. *Rúnaí Cúnta*
2. *Rúnaí*

Further to my minute of 25th instant the following gives the position regarding the points raised in the minute of 19.8.65 [sic] from A. Crn. [QMG] with some details as to prices and delivery dates in certain cases -

Para. 2a(i) 21 V.H.F. Mobile Radio Telephones (3 base and 18 substations). Pye Ireland had one base station and nine substations available and these have been ordered and are being collected... The sanction of Roinn Airgeadais [Dept. of Finance] for the balance has been sought.

2a (ii) The 20 H.F. Manpack Transmitter/Receivers were ordered on 22/8/69. These are in addition to the 197 sets already held of which 40 were purchased in 1968-69. Total requirements is 396. They cost £1,500 each. Delivery 10-12 weeks but some may be available in 2-3 weeks."

[The memorandum goes on to work through the list of required items, noting which have and have not been ordered. The mattresses, blankets etc. were on order and "efforts are being made to speed up deliveries. The Post Office had not placed an order for the full quantity of blankets as difficulty was being experienced in getting the colours required..." Supplies of Sleeping Bags, "Combat Boots" and other items are being expedited by the Post Office. As regards the warlike supplies it concludes:]

"7. The major items of Defensive Equipment in the current year's estimate are on order except the following:-

Subhead		
H.b(7)	F.N. Machine Guns	Tenders from Warnants are under examination by S. Ord. [Director of Ordnance]
H.6(16)	Anti Riot Grenades.	Tenders have been invited.

The attached statement shows the present position of ammunition supplies.

We are aware of alternative sources of supply for small arms ammunition and possibly some sources of 25 Pdr. ammunition but except for British sources for the latter the offers which we have had were not investigated. The offers for mortar ammunition from firms other than Brandt [French manufacturer] were not acceptable. The anti-tank ammunition has up to this been got from Sweden and we are not aware of any other firms who have developed ammunition to suit the Swedish guns we have.

Numerous requisitions for items for the troops in camps and refugee reception centres have been dealt with or are being handled as quickly as possible."

[NA S 650.]

Comment: I do not know why the Post Office was involved in the supplying process, but I am informed that this *was* the system.

Document 7: Minister Consulted On Martial Preparations, 3 September

[Memorandum to Minister Gibbons from Secretary Ó Cearnaigh/Kearney at the Department of Defence, dated 3rd September 1969 following up on the supply position:]

"Aire [Minister].

I think you should see the attached preliminary report prepared by the Contracts Officer on the Army's supply requirements as set out in the Quartermaster General's minute of 19th August.

The undermentioned items will be discussed with the Quartermaster General before any further action is taken towards their supply:-

Estimated Cost.

		£
3.	Barrack Services - Additional requirements.	95,000
4.	Sleeping Bags.	85,000
5b.	Marquees and Tents.	?
7d.	Respirators.	135,000

Regarding ammunition, the schedule gives particulars of the principal weapons held by the Defence Forces and the ammunition stocks available for them. The Quartermaster General's minute indicates that these stocks would suffice for only a few hours' to one or two days combat requirements.

The schedule also shows the stocks which for general planning purposes the military authorities consider should be available. These should theoretically meet 8 days' combat requirements. The cost would be about £16m. or, say, £2m. a day. The significance of these figures becomes apparent when it is realised that the total expenditure on weapons and ammunition (including maintenance) amounted to only £3,680,000 for the twelve years from 1957/58 to 1968/69.

All our ammunition comes from outside the country and many of the varieties have only one source of supply that we know of. (Small arms ammunition - 7.62 mm., 9 mm. and .303 [inch] - can be got from a number of sources). Under conditions where the Defence Forces would be involved in hostilities it would be reasonable to assume (a) that normal channels of supply would be interrupted by blockade and (b) that our regular Continental suppliers would, through diplomatic or other pressure, be prevented from fulfilling contracts for the Defence Forces.

Under the conditions envisaged, we would be dependant on (a) the stocks of ammunition we actually hold at the outbreak of hostilities and (b) such stocks as we could smuggle into the country by sea and air. For the latter we would have to rely on our own ingenuity and on the 'good offices' of international munition trafficers [sic] - a kind of underworld we have no experience of. All our suppliers are of the highest standing and, we assume, very much subject to the direction of their own governments.

The conclusion to be drawn is that stocks of weapons and ammunition must be built up in peace time to the maximum extent the country can afford.

As you know we wrote to the Department of Finance on 5th August about the provision to be made for 'capital' stores in the 1970/71 Estimate. The stores for which the military authorities sought provision included the following for ammunition:-

	Rounds.	£.
7.62 m/m ball (FN Rifle)	9,000,000	285,000
" " Tracer	2,000,000	94,000
84 m/m HEAT	4,000	130,000
" " HE	8,000	275,000
90 m/m HEAT	2,000	125,000
25 Pdr. HE	5,000	75,000
120 m/m Mortar HE	5,000	135,000
Hand Grenades	5,000	18,000
Tear Grenades	3,000	10,000
		£1,147,000"

[NA S 650.]

Comments: The Permanent Secretary at the Dept. of Defence is clearly taking very seriously the prospect of a Northern involvement for the Irish Army. His warning that stockpiles of armaments would be advisable is significant. The fact that his memorandum is for his Minister shows that James Gibbons was fully implicated in the preparations for possible hostilities.

The nine million rounds of ammunition listed as needed for FN rifles seems rather a lot for the 250-300 infantry listed in Document One, but would be more in keeping with the need to prepare for intervention North of the Border. We are talking of 90 lorry loads.

The two million tracer bullets are for use in machine guns during night operations. They enable the soldier to see where the bullets are flying (but also enable the opponent to locate firing positions).

We have already noted the purposes for which HE and HEAT ammunition can be used. All that need be remarked is that the quantities suggested allow for considerable operations.

The Tear Grenades can be used in riot situations.

This memorandum within the Department of Defence envisages logistical preparations for engagements lasting at least a week.

I do not know what "capital" stores are.

(It is striking that Ireland, which at that time had a reasonable manufacturing capacity, had no facilities to produce even the simplest bullet. During the Jewish Palestine war against Britain of 1945-7 the insurgents had extensive secret arms factories. It must be assumed that Ireland failed to develop a defence industry by secret arrangement with Britain.)

[An 11-column table, entitled *Defensive Equipment*, is attached to this document, showing the position with regard to various weapons: stocks held, requirements, what is on order, the price, financial deficiency, delivery times and other remarks. It is reproduced below, on pages 38 and 39.]

Type of Weapon	No. of Weapons held.	AMMUNITION Requirements	Holding	On Order	Deficiency	Price (current)
25 Pdr	48	145,000	18,000	2,600	124,500	12-5.0
Mortars 120 mm	72	112,000	15,000	-	97,000	24-0-0
81 mm	201	235,000 HE	63,000	-	172,000	18-0-0 (a)
		45,000 Smoke	14,000	-	31,000	18-0-0 (a)
60 mm	199	235,000 HE	15,000	-	220,000	13.10-0 (a)
		45,000 Smoke	6,500	-	38,500	13-10-0 (a)
Anti Tank 84 mm	447	45,000 Heat	10,000	3,600	31,400	27-15-0
		20,000 H.E.	2,500	-	17,500	33-0-0
90mm	96	10,000 Heat	1,900	-	8,100	66-0-0
		5,000 H.E.	-	-	5,000	75-0-0 (a)
A.A. 40 mm L70	2	12,000 H.E. 500 APCBC.	7,500	-	5,000	8-10-0 (a)
40 mm L60	24	-	99,000			
M.G. Vickers .303	505	8,600,000	12,000,000		43,000,000	£37000 per M
Light Bren.303	2,375	9,500,000				
Rifles .303	50,000	37,500,000				
Sub Machine Guns						
Gustav 9 mm	13,800	17,500,000	18,000,000		-	
Rifles F.N. 7.62	9,386	7,000,000	9,000,000	2,000,000	1,000,000	£33700 per M
MAG762 without mountings	300	5,000,000 (b)				
Hand Grenades		250,000	6,500	-	243,500	£3-7-6
Anti Riot Grenades	-	10,000	3,000	2,000*	5,000	£3-1-0

(b) This figure is calculated pro rata to Vicker MGs.

(a) Price is only approx.

Total cost of deficiency of ammunition

Quartermaster's Defensive

Total value Deficiency	Delivery Time		
	Commence	Complete	
£			
1,530,000	4 months	2-3 years	
2,328,000	3 months	2-3 years	
3,096,000	3 months	3-4 years	
558,000	3 "	1 year	
2,970,000	3 "	2-3 years	
520,000	3 "	1 year	
871,000	6 "	1-2 years	
577,000	6 "	1-2 years	
535,000	6 "	1-2 years	
375,000	6 "	1-2 years	
42,000	7 "	1 year	Obsolescent
			These guns are manually operated and are obsolete.
1,581,000	5 "	3 years	When the MAGs 7.62 are obtained the requirement for these MGs will disappear.
			Requirements of ammunition for rifles may be over estimated in view of change over to F.N. rifles.
-	-	-	
34,000	5 "	6 months	Tenders are under examination for 100 MAGs 7.62. Mountings for 500 are on order. Delivery over 2 years. Purchase of 100 MAGs is proposed for 1970-71.
882,000	End of 1970	2-3 years	No stocks available from British M.O.D. Supplies may be available at end of 1970.
15,000	2 months	4 months	* Tenders have been invited for 2,000 grenades. Delivery 10 weeks.
15,844,000			

Equipment Report, end August 1969

Document 8: Planning Board On NI Operations: Interim Report, 27 September

[On 27th September 1969 the *Planning Board On Northern Ireland Operations* based in the Chief of Staff's Branch, produced a document signed by Lt. Col. E.S. De Barra/Barry, Comdt. G. Ó Suilleabhán/Gerry O'Sullivan and Comdt. Ó Ceallaigh/ Kevin P. Kelly. The document has SECRET typed at the top and bottom of each page, as well as each being rubber-stamped *Secret*. This is its *Interim Report*:]

" SCS 29

SECRET

Oifig an Chinn Fóirne.
[Office of Chief of Staff]
27 Meán Fómhair, 1969.
Copy No. 1

Interim Report of Planning Board
on Northern Ireland Operations

Object.

1. To report on the feasibility of the Defence Forces undertaking military combat or support operations in Northern Ireland, including the nature and implications of such operations.

2. Limitations on object.

a. The board would have liked a clearly defined political objective. In the absence of such an objective the board considered a number of political situations each of which might suggest military intervention.

b. Psychologically the Defence Forces are oriented on defence (including offensive defensive operations).

c. There is no precise knowledge available at this stage to the Board as to what the reaction of public opinion would be either North or South of the Border to offensive action on the part of the Defence Forces in Northern Ireland. Such reaction was not therefore considered as a factor though it could have considerable influence on the outcome of any operations so undertaken.

d. All situations visualised assume that military action would be taken unilaterally by the Defence Forces and would meet with hostility from Northern Ireland Security Forces.

Situations considered.

3. The following political situations were considered.

a. Attacks on the Catholic minority by Protestant extremists with which the Northern Ireland Security Forces cannot cope (SITUATION A).

b. Conflict between the Catholic minority and the Northern Ireland Security Forces on Civil Rights issues. (SITUATION B).

c. Conflict between Republican-Nationalist elements (possibly supported by illegal elements from South of the Border) and the Northern Ireland Security Forces. (SITUATION C).

d. Conflict between Protestant extremists and Northern Ireland security forces not directly involving the minority. (SITUATION D).

Summary of conclusions drawn from a consideration of the factors bearing on our objective.

4. As a basis for the development of feasible courses of action the following conclusions were drawn from a study of the factors bearing on our objective.

a. The Defence Forces have NO capability of embarking on unilateral military operation, of any kind (either conventional or unconventional), from a firm base at home. This means, in effect, that were operations in any form to be launched into Northern Ireland we would be exposed to the threat of retaliatory punitive military action by United Kingdom forces on the Republic. Therefore any operations undertaken against Northern Ireland would be militarily unsound.

b. The Defence Forces have no capability to engage successfully in conventional offensive military operations against the security forces in Northern Ireland at unit or higher level.

c. Accepting the implications of subpara 4a. above, conventional military operations on a small scale up to a maximum of company level, and unconventional operations, could be undertaken by the Defence Forces subject to action being taken as outlined in subpara 4d. following.

d. The provision of forces capable of carrying out operations as outlined in subpara 4c. would generally speaking require changes in the organisation, dispositions, training and motivation of the Defence Forces as they exist at present.

e. In addition to action as outlined in subpara 4c. above, the Defence forces would also be capable of the following, taken separately or together.

(1) Organising and conducting military training in the Republic for nationalists living in Northern Ireland.

(2) Supplying arms, ammunition and equipment in accordance with availability to nationalist elements in Northern Ireland.

This type of action would involve relatively minor planning and training problems.

f. The existence of a common border with Northern Ireland and a good road net facilitates cross border operations. However, in the light of modern surveillance techniques available to the security forces in the North, guerrilla operations in Northern Ireland would be difficult to conduct over a protracted period.

g. Key areas, politically, are BELFAST, DERRY, STRABANE, OMAGH, ENNISKILLEN, DUNGANNON, NEWRY and ARMAGH. From the point of view military operations [in ?] DERRY, STRABANE, ENNISKILLEN and NEWRY are most suitable by virtue of their proximity to the Border.

h. The majority of the more important vital installations in Northern Ireland. e.g., BELFAST Airport, T.V. Studios, Docks and main industries are located in the NE corner, some distance from the Border. Any military operations conducted against these should preferably be of the unconventional type.

Feasible courses, militarily, under each of the political situations outlined in para 3 (Courses listed are in all cases subject to limitations listed in para 4 above).

5. Situation A [Protestant attacks on Catholics]

a. To conduct conventional operations at coy [company] level with one or more companies directed at objectives located in key areas such as DERRY and NEWRY.

b. A wide range of unconventional operations in any part of Northern Ireland designed to draw forces off from the area of direct conflict.

c. Supply of arms, ammunition, equipment, and medical supplies to Catholic minority in accordance with availability.

6. Situation B [Catholics v. NI Security Forces]

a. To conduct conventional operations up to coy level directly at Northern Ireland Security Forces.

b. In conjunction with 'a' above, conventional operations up to coy level directed at key areas along the Border designed to draw Security Forces away from the area of direct conflict.

c. A wide range of unconventional operations in any part of Northern Ireland designed to draw forces off from the area of direct conflict independently or in conjunction with a. and b. above.

d. In conjunction with a. and b. and c. above, the supply of arms, ammunition, equipment and medical supplies to Catholic minority, in accordance with availability.

7. Situation C [Republicans-Nationalists + Southern Illegals v. NI Security Forces]

Courses as for SITUATION B plus the following:

Organising training for Nationalist-Republican elements.

8. Situation D [Protestant extremists v. NI Security Forces]

a. Infiltrate elements armed and equipped to org, train and advise Catholic and Nationalist groups in vulnerable areas far from the Border (e.g. BELFAST).

b. Deploy sub-units up to coy level across the Border prepared to keep routes open for refugees moving South.

Summary of points emerging from an analysis of Courses of Action under the various situations.

9. All but one of the courses considered are offensive in nature. The degree of success of these courses would be limited by the psychological influence of the traditional concept of the Defence Forces as an organisation with a mission concerned primarily with the Defence of the country.

10. In the case of conventional operations, all courses would preclude the selection of deep objectives and would concentrate on those close to the Border. In addition it is considered that individual operations could be of limited duration only.

11. Training and operational preparedness demanded by all of these courses is adversely affected by

a. the extent to which our existing resources have been committed to administration.

b. the degree of dispersion of units and personnel of the Permanent Defence Force.

c. the multiplicity of Staffs headquarters and units in the PDF.

d. the fact that the regular infantry battalions, which together make up the key element involved are particularly low in strength (34.7% of establishment strength).

e. the relative unsuitability of the organisation and establishments of the Permanent Defence Force for combat operations.

f. extra military employment of the Defence Forces, such as film-making.

12. It is considered that the present standard of training of both individuals and units is inadequate to meet the requirements of offensive oriented courses.

There is a need to embark on a general training programme designed to prepare the Defence Forces to undertake such operations. This will include inter alia, physical fitness, individual combat, a very high standard of weapon skills and tactical training up to and including company level, as well as specialised skills required for unconventional operations such as demolitions, communications, street fighting and riot control.

13. It is considered that conventional operations, even at company level, would be hazardous in the absence of APCs [Armoured Personnel Carriers], fighter aircraft and air defence weapons.

14. In the context of offensive operations it cannot be assumed that the morale of the Defence Forces is high. Esprit d'Corps [sic] is virtually non-existent in the Infantry Corps which in the present situation would be a key element. Although leadership material is adequate, the lack of combat experience, and even tactical training, means that our leadership resources have not been fully developed.

15. Notwithstanding what is said in para 14, it is possible that in the event of units of the Defence Forces being sent to intervene in the North, the motivation generated in going to assist ones countrymen, might bring about an increase in individual and unit morale.

16. The adoption of a mission involving "Active intervention in Northern Ireland" would demand an intensive intelligence effort oriented on the mission, and both before and during operations.

17. A number of the courses suggested, would involve support of and cooperation with various movements in Northern Ireland such as Civil Rights and Republican Groups. This could also lead to cooperation with illegal groups in the Republic. These contacts would have serious political implications on the national and international scene. They could also pose serious problems in the aftermath, particularly where arms and equipment have been supplied.

18. Notwithstanding the implications of para 17, it is considered that the support and assistance of a substantial part of the minority would be essential for success in Defence Force operations in Northern Ireland. The fact that active intervention by us in the North, would expose the minority to retaliatory action could limit the amount of overt assistance they would be prepared to give.

19. It would be necessary to confine conventional operations in those areas where there is a Catholic/Nationalist majority. In minority areas, particularly BELFAST, only unconventional operations could be conducted. It is considered also that it is to these latter areas that supplies of arms and equipment should be chiefly directed.

20. The involvement of the Defence Forces in operations in Northern Ireland will lessen the extent to which they can provide resources for the security of vital civil and military installations in the Republic. The extent to which the security of these installations might be compromised would depend on the reaction of

a. The British Government (would they direct military attacks against the Republic?).

b. The extremist Protestants (would they engage in sabotage or direct attacks on Border towns?).

c. The subversive groups or 'loyalist' elements in the Republic (would they take advantage of our preoccupation in the North to initiate action towards the attainment of their own objectives South of the Border?).

21. Intervention in Northern Ireland will involve a number of diverse actions ranging from control of operations (including training and supply operations) to planning functions at CCA [Army HQ]. This will involve the setting up of acceptable command structures at all operational levels, and also an element at CCA to affect coordination of planning activities in all three military Branches.

<u>Recommendations</u>

22. <u>General</u>. It emerges from an analysis of the situation (Paras 9 to 21 inclusive) that there are certain specific actions which require to be taken now in order to prepare the Defence Forces for active intervention in Northern Ireland should this be decided upon. There are also other considerations included in these paras which will require to be borne in mind when operational and other plans are being developed for the implementation of the courses of action. The recommendations set out below are directed towards the immediate action to be taken.

23. The Board recommends that:

a. a command structure be established to plan, organise, direct, coordinate and control operations in Northern Ireland, and that the structure be the subject of a separate study.

b. a minimum of one infantry battalion in each Command area be brought up to full establishment strength as soon as possible and organised trained and equipped to operate in company groups, and that the Planning Staff, P&O [Planning & Operations] be required to prepare a suitable battalion organisation to meet these requirements.

c. The three motor squadrons to be brought up to establishment strength.

d. A Special Forces Unit, prepared for employment, primarily, on unconventional operations be organised, trained and equipped in CTC [Curragh Training Camp]; the organisation establishment of this Unit to be the subject of a separate study.

e. because of the training deficiencies and requirements reflected in the body of this report, an intensive training programme be initiated without delay by S/Trn [Director of Training] to provide for the tactical proficiency of the units referred to in b, c and d above.

f. officer training be oriented on operational situations in a Northern Ireland setting.

g. the desirability of supporting the minority in the North by training and by the supply of arms and equipment be considered, and if found to be acceptable, the development of plans for the implementation of these courses.

h. the intelligence in the North be intensified and directed towards the courses of action suggested.

j. with regard to procurement policies, priority be given to the purchase of APCs [Armoured Personnel Carriers], air defence weapons and riot control and demolition equipment.

k. a motivation programme be initiated aimed at indoctrinating our own troops.

24. The Board considers it necessary to draw attention to the following
a. the provision of troops on the scale visualised will require a study of the present administrative commitments, dispositions and multiplicity of units (including Border deployments) and may involve the suspension of certain units and the closing of some posts,
b. the commitments in connection with operations in Northern Ireland will mean a diminution in the forces available for security and this problem will have to be met by an acceptance of the risk involved or by the call-up on permanent service of FCA elements.
c. there is a requirement to suspend all extra-military employment of the Defence Forces."

[NA 29; Comdt. Gerry O'Sullivan was subsequently to become a Chief of Staff; there is no point *23.i.*.]

Comments: I have not found the chain of command setting up this Planning Board For Northern Ireland operations. It can confidently be assumed, however, that there was a Government decision establishing it. The report was compiled in the Office of the Chief of Staff. It envisages that the Director of Planning and Operations (Colonel John C. O'Donovan), should prepare a suitable battalion organisation to meet requirements. The Director of Training (Colonel Daniel Fitzgerald) is to initiate an intensive Training Programme without delay. (I have also seen Colonel John Donovan mentioned as Director of Training.)

The Planning Board is referred to above in *Exercise Armageddon*. As we shall see in later documents, the reports it produced were circulated in a narrow circle, and submitted to the officers attending the meeting of the Council for Defence of 13th October. This meeting was chaired by Defence Minister Gibbons, and attended by the Parliamentary Secretary to the Department of Defence, Desmond O'Malley.

Whilst cautious about direct Army involvement North of the Border, the report is very clear that the Army could help the minority in two ways: training nationalists and supplying weaponry (*4e, 1. and 2*; *19*; *23.h.*). We know for a fact that these proposals were implemented. Chapters in this pamphlet provide evidence for training of Northern civilians and the supply of weaponry. The Irish Government also set up a substantial Relief Fund, which was used for welfare and warfare (defensive).

Paragraph *23.g.* is the most crucial in the whole document. It calls on the Government to consider training and arming the Northern Ireland minority. Here is direct evidence to confirm that Captain Kelly was not acting independently and subversively in 1969-70.

There are a number of striking points in this Interim Report. The Army complains that it was given no clearly-defined political objective. Perhaps that is because the Cabinet itself did not have one. Pamphlet One in this series, describing Ireland's only appeal to the United Nations in 1969, showed poor strategic planning at Cabinet level.

Paragraph *2.b.* report of the Planning Board On Northern Ireland Operations makes it clear that the Army had been asked to consider offensive operations for the first time.

The four political scenarios on which military action are predicated were realistic.

Situation *3.a.*, in which Northern Ireland security forces could not cope with Protestant disorder, was a dream scenario for the Irish Government. It would then be called in to assist the Northern Ireland security forces.

Paragraph *3.c.* contemplates Irish Army involvement in conflict between the Northern Ireland security forces and the minority.

Paragraph *7.* envisages that there could be cooperation with irregular elements: *"Republicans-Nationalists + Southern Illegals against NI Security Forces"*.

Paragraph 4a emphasises the vulnerability of the Republic to counter-action to any major offensive North of the Border, but subsequent paragraphs seem to suggest that Company-level and unconventional Army actions would be less hazardous for the hinterland. The implication of these remarks is that the Planning Board was recommending operations requiring deployments of 70-90 men. And to undertake even this, special units would have to be put together and given training. Recommendation 23d, proposing the setting up of a special force, was consonant with the recent formation of a Rangers element.

Closer military involvement with the North required the development of an active Intelligence capacity (paragraphs 16, *23.h*). This was done, with Captain Kelly and up to eleven other Military Intelligence Officers deployed on Northern duties. There may have been other initiatives too. Taoiseach's Department files contain long eye-witness reports from Seamus Brady, as well as other unsigned detailed reports which may have originated from the Department of Justice.

The suggestion that Army morale was poor is not borne out by other sources, though it may have applied to the more senior officers. The rank and file of the Army was anxious for action.

In his search for evidence to vindicate his own role with regard to the North, Captain Kelly also found this document in the Archives and made various pencil notes on his own copy. He noted against point *'8a'* above ("Infiltrate elements armed and equipped to org, train and advise Catholic and Nationalist groups in vulnerable areas far from the Border (e.g. BELFAST)": *"My job to pinpoint such 'elements'"*. Captain Kelly also marked *"N.B."* against the proposal to supply *"military training"*, *"arms, ammunition and equipment... to nationalist elements in Northern Ireland"* above, and again against the suggestion of *"military operations... of the unconventional type"* against Northern Ireland *"installations"* away from Border areas.

A retired Army officer who was asked to comment on this Chapter states of Point *23.3.*, recommending special training:

"Before the establishment of the Rangers, courses were run in the Infantry

School, The Military College, for classes (20-30) of young officers, who were given training in infiltration and minor tactics—the strategy, apparently, was based upon small units infiltrating and operating in Northern Ireland—the protection of the minority, by them, was, I believe, an over-riding factor. They used the name, Fiann Óglaig, or Volunteer Fianna—a fore-runner of the Rangers. They, in turn, would train others when they returned to their units."

This document is extraordinarily important in vindicating the innocence of Captain Kelly and others criminalised by Taoiseach Lynch in May 1970.

It should be said that, while the Army was acting on its remit from the Cabinet to consider practicalities of offensive military action to aid the Northern minority, Jack Lynch was sending out conciliatory signals to Britain. He made a speech on 17th September 1969 which *Hibernia* took as modifying his fighting talk of 13th August (see *Ireland's Only Appeal To The United Nations*, p70). However, this speech did not have the same status as the television address to the nation and it made no change to the covert policy of preparing to give military assistance to the Northern Ireland minority.

(*Note On Army Organisation:* I am informed that a Section is two Corporals with 8 Privates; a Platoon is a Lieutenant, one Sergeant, and a Private (Runner) and three Privates (60mm Mortar team), plus 3 Sections; a Company is a Commandant (equivalent to a Major in the British Army), with a small Company Headquarters and three Platoons (140 approximately). It may be augmented. It can also be referred to as a Rifle Company. A Battalion, under a Lt. Colonel, has a Battalion Headquarters, with a Headquarters Company, and 3 or 4 Companies, with one Support Company with heavier weapons: around 500 to 700 troops in all. The Headquarters Company contains cooks and bottle-washers etc.; and the Support Company will have 81 mm Mortars, Medium Machine Guns, and Anti-Tank-guns. There are—outside a Battalion—other types of Companies, but in the document above, it is Rifle or Infantry Companies that are being referred to.

Motor Squadrons, also known as Cavalry Squadrons, have armoured cars, *not* tanks; they are used to seize and hold; for flank protection; or for reconnaissance, harassment, and delay of an enemy. Mobility and flexibility are their *forte*.

A Captain can be a No. 2 in a Company, but can also be the No. 1. There are Captains all the way up the scale. An Adjutant performs secretarial functions in the British Army. In the Irish Army the Adjutant General is the Number 2 and the Quartermaster General is the No. 3. The Chief of Staff is the No. 1. At the time in question, Lt. General was the highest position in the Irish Army.

In military writing, some things, to avoid ambiguity, are printed in script or put in capitals in type, e.g. all negatives, names, place-names, compass points.

If 'Secret' is used in a military document, it *has* to be put at the top and bottom of each page.)

Document 9: Special Cross-Border Command Structure, 8 October

[An "Annex" has been released which appears to have been produced on 8th October 1969. It is mentioned in the Report below at *f.b.* and may also be the *"command structure"* referred to in paragraph *23.a.* above. This sets out the staff requirements for Cross-Border operations. The document has <u>SECRET</u> typed at the top and bottom of each page, as well as each being rubber-stamped *Secret*:]

" SCS 29

SECRET

Annex A to
Staff Study dated 8 D. Fómh 69.

Suggested organisation of Special Planning Staff for Border Operations.

OIC
[Officer In Charge]
(Colonel)

Ops	Int	A	Q	Adm Staff
Lt Col Comdt Capt	Lt Col Comdt (Sigs) Capt	(Comdt) Capt	(Comdt) Capt	Capt Sgt. Clerk Sgt Draughts-man

[Abbreviations: Ops-Operations; Int-Intelligence; A-Adjutancy; Q-Quartermastering (supply); Adm-Administration; Sigs-Signals]

Explanatory Notes

1. The Staff would be found from the existing establishments of elements NOT directly involved in Border operations. Its function would be the planning of all aspects of Border operations at CCA level.

2. The Staff would provide the nucleus of a HQ to conduct cross Border operations should these be embarked upon. This would involve an increase in the establishments recommended. The increase required in such circumstances would be the subject of a study by the Staff itself.

3. The 'A' and 'Q' representatives are visualised as having a relatively minor role in the planning stage and would in effect be liaison officers between their respective Branches and the Special Planning Staff.

4. Primary function and Personnel

a. Ops The preparation of contingency operational plans within the context of the courses visualised in Interim Report dated 27 M. Fómh 69, and in accordance with any political guidance which may be given relative to the political situations visualised in the same report. The personnel for this sub-element should be based on the Planning Staff of P70 [Planning & Operations] Section supplemented by suitable personnel from outside of P70.

b. Int The development of an intelligence system which would provide intelligence support for any operations embarked upon. The production of intelligence estimates as a basis for the development of operational plans. The personnel for this sub-element should come partly from the current strength of the Intelligence Section at CCA [Army HQ] supplemented by other intelligence trained personnel as available.

c. 'A' and 'Q' It is visualised that the A and Q functions would not be great initially and that the Planning Officers from the respective Branches at CCA would operate on call providing adm and log [administrative and logistical] information as required. The presence on the Special Planning Staff of a Captain from each Branch is considered desirable to operate in a liaison role in the production of this information.

d. Adm Staff A Captain is considered necessary to handle the various adm problems which will arise in the typing of material, the production of sketches and maps and for maintaining a filing system. He will require the assistance of a Sgt Clerk and a Sgt Draughtsman."

[NA SCS 29.]

Comment: This document appears to propose that a multi-disciplinary planning group be established at Army Headquarters to prepare cross-Border missions.

Document Ten: Conduct Of Cross-Border Operations

[The Planning Board for Northern Ireland Operations (Officers De Barra, Ó Suilleabhán, and C. Ó Ceallaigh, based in the Chief of Staff's Branch) produced a further Report now released into the public domain. Again the document has SECRET typed at the top and bottom of each page, as well as each being rubber-stamped *Secret*, and is dated 10th October 1969:]

" SCS 29

SECRET

Oifig an Chinn Fóirne,
CCA.
10 D. Fómh 69
Copy No 1.

SUBJECT: Planning for and conduct of Border operations.

1. PROBLEM. To determine the most suitable command and staff structure in connection with the planning for and conduct of Border operations as visualised in Interim Report dated 27 M. Fómh [Sept.] 69 and to make recommendations.

2. FACTS BEARING ON THE PROBLEM

a. The nature of the operations visualised and the distances involved suggest maximum delegation to lower level operating units and the exercise of flexible and loose control by CCA [Army HQ] and Commands.

b. The relative dependence on civil line communications makes direct control of Border operations by CCA and Commands difficult.

c. The setting up of mobile CCA and Command tactical headquarters would decrease the dependence on civil communications and reduce the requirement for delegation to lower levels of command.

d. Logistical and administrative support of Border operations will be effected by Commands.

e. Troops operating in DONEGAL could be isolated by British action across the Border from BELEEK to seize BALLYSHANNON. This would cut DONEGAL off from the REPUBLIC though communication by radio could be maintained and supply could probably be effected by sea.

f. As far as the conduct of Border operations is concerned it would be desirable to operate within the provisions of A18.

g. CCA is not adequately staffed to embark on detailed planning in connection with Border operations.

h. Only Ceann O and Ceann I [Commanders of Eastern and Western Commands] are directly involved in Border operations from the planning and conduct of operations point of view. Elements not directly involved such as Ceann D [Southern Command] and CTC [Curragh Training Camp] could possibly make officers available to CCA [Army HQ] to supplement planning staffs there.

j. Because of the extent of the planning to be carried out at CCA in connection with Border operations a special staff would need to be employed composed of personnel from all the Branches at CCA. The activities of the Planning Sub-Section, P70 should be dovetailed with this.

k. In the event of operations being conducted it would be desirable that this planning staff would become the CCA Command and Staff (or Field Forces Headquarters) conducting the operation. For this reason the planning staff should be a 'high-powered' one. It should also be provided with suitable accommodation.

l. Command Staffs are capable of embarking on the preparation of operational and administrative support plans on the basis of missions and guidance to be given by CCA.

m. Command Staff are capable of managing all operations visualised particularly unconventional and support operations (supply and training).

3. DISCUSSION

a. It is clear that subject to missions and guidance from CCA, Commands should plan for and conduct all Border operations. CCA should be satisfied to exercise loose control of such operations with maximum power being given to unit commanders. If this is not acceptable it would be necessary to deploy a Field Forces Headquarters forward of DUBLIN and also to deploy tactical headquarters forward in the case of Ceann O and Ceann I [Eastern and Western Commands]. In general the command structure should be as provided for in A.18 with some modification.

b. Because of the relative vulnerability of DONEGAL plans should be prepared to provide for the continued existence there of our units should the area be isolated by British action. These plans should include provision for the elements there to be combined in a separate sub-command should such isolation take place.

c. The importance of unit commanders in such operations suggests that these commanders should be selected and introduced to the problem as early as possible.

d. The detailed planning required at CCA level should be embarked upon without delay. The staff involved should be 'high-powered' and should be capable of manning the Field Forces Headquarters should operations commence. It should include representatives of all three Branches at CCA.

e. The operations and intelligence officers in Ceann O and Ceann I should be briefed without delay and instructed to initiate broad planning on the basis of information available.

4. ACTION RECOMMENDED

a. That command structure as provided for in A.18 should be employed with the possibility that minor modifications might be required (e.g. the possibility of setting up a sub-command in DONEGAL).

b That a special staff be established at CCA to prepare studies and plans in connection with possible Border operations and that liaison be established between this body and the Planning Sub-Section of P&O which should be briefed without delay. The special staff be sufficiently high-powered to meet the requirements of its becoming a Field Forces Headquarters should this be required. (A suggested organisation is attached at Annex 'A').

c. That the basement at DOD [Dept. of Defence ?] be equipped as a headquarters and that the special planning staff commence work there.

d. That unit commanders to command the three battalions and the Special Forces Unit be selected and that they be introduced to the problem and given contingency missions.

e. That operations and intelligence staffs at Ceann O and Ceann I be briefed on the present situation and given missions and planning guidance."

[NA SCS 29. A.18 refers to the Defence Force Regulation laying down the Army structure; *Point 3.d.* speaks of three Branches at Army Headquarters: these would be Operations, Adjutancy and Quartermastering, but if Intelligence is added, that would make four.]

Comments: The thrust of these proposals is that possible military objectives should be handed out to designated officers, who should start studying the problems involved, in case they are called upon to act.

I am not sure of DOD stood for Department of Defence. If it did, that would confirm that this contingency planning was directly under the authority of Government.

While overall control was to be centralised, the suggestion was that there would be some devolution of authority and forward or mobile command posts.

The Report makes clear that, far from Government military policy scaling down as the August events receded and the British Army took control of security in the North, the new military approach was taking shape and becoming more definite. The proposal is that broad planning should start immediately.

This report is dated 10th October 1969—a few days after Captain Kelly met Citizens' Defence activists in Bailieboro to discuss steps to be taken to provide for Catholic defence, including cooperation with the Irish Army. That Bailieboro meeting dovetails with the Planning Board recommendations, which make particular mention of "supply and training" of the minority (see *2.m.* above).

Furthermore Paragraph *3.e.* above specifically mentions the involvement of Army Intelligence. As personal assistant to Colonel Hefferon (Director of Military Intelligence), Captain Kelly was the most senior officer deployed in such duties.

As to the scale of Army deployment, paragraph *4.d.* envisages the involvement of three battalions and a Special Forces Unit. On my reckoning this amounts to over 1,500 troops. But, as the document makes clear, there would be no 'invasion'—just particular missions.

The head of Eastern Command at the time was Col. P.J. Hally, Colonel Christopher E. Shortall was in Charge of Western Command, Col. Carl O'Sullivan headed Southern Command, and the Commandant of Curragh Training Camp was Colonel James J. Quinn.

At this period there was a siege air in many Catholic areas in Belfast, and there were reasonable grounds for expecting Protestant armed resistance to changes in the administration of Northern Ireland. And, just nine days after this report, Northern paramilitaries came close to blowing up Ballyshannon Power Station in Co. Donegal.

Given what was revealed in these files, one wonders about "Document No. 1", dated 6th October, removed from Military Intelligence File 5/A before it was given over to the National Archive. This and several other documents are flagged as withheld from public release.

Document 11: Critique Of Proposals For NI Operations. 13 October

[A commentary on the Reports of the Planning Board appears in a document dated 13th October, issuing from *"Rng P0, CCA"* [Planning and Operations Section]. It was produced with some urgency so that the Army command troika could consider it before the Council of Defence met. The letters *a,b,d,* etc. below comment on the points in paragraph 2 of the Planning Board recommendations above (Document 10). The copy in the file is unsigned, but may be by Col. J. Adams:]

" <u>SECRET</u>

<u>SCS 29</u>
Rng P70,
CCA.

<u>Recommendations of Planning Board</u>

The reports of the Board were not available for sufficient time to permit a detailed study of the conclusions and recommendations. Accordingly the comments hereunder cannot be considered as fully comprehensive and are submitted as an interim measure to meet the needs of the General Staff for the Council of Defence Meeting to be held at 1500 hours on 15/10/69.

<u>Recommendations of the Board</u>

a. <u>The command structure to be set up within the terms of DFR A.18.</u>

Comment

(1) Military action must be geared to political decision. Only in Army HQ can the necessary dovetailing of military and political factors be undertaken. This requires that the Chief of Staff be given a command function over the entire operation which is in conflict with the present structure. This could be overcome by a broad written directive from the Minister.

(2) The concept of a separate planning staff in Army HQ cuts across existing organisation and is not desirable in broad principle. However the inadequacy of staff particularly in Plans and Operations and Intelligence and the need to ensure secrecy in such operations may make the step necessary. Ideally the organisation of Army HQrs should have a planning division consisting of planning elements from all three branches.

b. The provision of one inf [infantry] battalion and one mot [motor] squadron in each command.

Comment

(1) Ideally it is very much better to maintain the seven battalions of the Forces at recommended establishment than to build up one battalion from each Command at the expense of the remainder. (The recommendations of the Defence Review Board Report are valid in this respect).

(2) With present strength and even by adding personnel from administrative and support arms, it would not be possible to put three infantry battalions and three motor squadrons on the border in an organisation which could be considered as combat effective. The minimum combat effective establishments for a battalion and cavalry squadron are as follows:-

	Offrs	NCOs	Men	Total
One Bn	32	183	522	737
One Cav Sqn	10	46	146	202
	42	229	668	939
For three Commands	126	587	2,004	2,817

The present strength of the Combat Units is as follows:-

	Offrs	NCOs	Men	Total
Inf	101	440	808	1,349
Cav	43	119	176	338
	193	713	1,230	2,136

Thus there is a considerable short-fall of strength. The capabilities of the Forces would depend to the extent of recruiting otherwise, the demand on Commands should hardly exceed a large reinforced company or at most a group [sic].

[There is no point c.]

d. Organisation of Special Forces Units

Comment

(1) While CTC [Curragh Training Camp] could be the main training base for a special operations force, the personnel required for this type of force would have to be young, fit and highly trained. CTC would not be able from its own resources to find personnel for this type of unit and would have to draw on personnel from other Commands thus adding to the existing short-fall.

(2) The present course output will be approximately 160 all ranks. It is visualised however that the Officer and NCO output from the present course would be used as instructors on courses in Commands to provide a large nucleus of specially trained personnel throughout the forces.

e. Training Deficiencies and Requirements

Comment It can be assumed that the troops would have completed basic training. Priorities would then be

Night training
Tactical training
Training of specialists - Mortar men, Intelligence, Field Engineering, Signals etc.

Once the troops have assembled there would be no major problem. At least one month of intensive training would be required.

f. Officer training to be oriented towards N.I. situation,

Comment

Such a development would require clearance from the Government as the political implications and the danger of leakage would be serious. Closer cooperation with nationalist organisations across the Border would be needed in order to provide the type of information envisaged.

g. Supporting the minority in the North by training and by supply of arms and equipment.

Comment

(1) The number of persons of the minority in the NORTH who would be prepared to take an active part against the security forces in N. Ireland is not known. It may be assumed however that the number is NOT great.

(2) Much of the activity recommended in the report e.g.

(f) Officer training oriented to situations in N. Ireland
(k) Indoctrination of troops

could not be carried out on a widespread basis without a leakage of intentions to the public and press. In present circumstances this might clearly conflict with the will of the Government.

(3) The recommendations to form one full strength battalion in each Command would seriously weaken the capability of other units and would not provide an expansion base for them. In this connection there is no feasible alternative to the recommendations of the Defence Review Board Report and the views of the General Staff in regard to the organisation of the Defence Forces.

Sustained operations of this nature would demand the total commitment of the

State and it would be foolhardy to attempt it without very careful planning and support. Should the operation miscarry, the consequences could be very grave for the State and the people it is intended to assist.

The minimum commitment would be to bring the PDF up to estab strength without delay. Procurement of the necessary equipment and ammunition and a realistic review of the FCA to include its organisation training facilities and conditions of service."

[NA SCS 29; 'PDF' is the Permanent Defence Force, i.e., the Regular Army, and 'estab' is establishment.]

Comments: The way the Irish Army was organised was intended to facilitate a rapid expansion in times of crisis. That is to say, it was top-heavy with ranks. Of the Regular Army something like three quarters had rank.

The Irish Army was also decentralised, with separate vertical Commands around the country. This complicated the devising of arrangements for action in the North, as did the fact that the Army was seriously under strength.

Existing arrangements were geared to coping with a major crisis, such as the Second World War, or with small deployments, such as with the United Nations. But the decentralisation of skills and scattering of combat troops around the country in a situation where there was an overall shortage presented difficulties when medium-scale operations needed to be mounted in a hurry.

The Planning Board On Northern Ireland Operations had recommended that active formations be established, cannibalising the Commands around the country. The Planning And Operations Section was countering with the proposal that the Army be brought up to strength.

While the Planning Board was putting forward positive proposals to enable military action to occur, this critique noted the difficulties in the way of such action.

However, in one respect this Report is spot on. Point *a. (1)* above takes issue with the Planning Board proposal that the new army formation be arranged according to Defence Regulation *A.18*. This provides for the decentralisation of authority to the troika (Chief of Staff, Adjutant-General, Quartermaster-General). What this critique proposes instead is that the Minister for Defence override these divisions with a Directive giving the Chief of Staff overall command responsibility. The implication of this is that the Chief of Staff should effectively be made Commander in Chief (under the Minister for Defence), a move which would facilitate military action.

It will be noted that this report was produced hurriedly in order that the troika be fully briefed for a Council for Defence meeting on 15th October (see below). The minutes for this meeting which I found were dated 13th October. It is possible that the Council for Defence meeting was brought forward a couple of days.

Point *b.(2)* envisages the deployment of greater strengths that those I estimate above. The reference to special training of *"mortar men"* in *(2) e.* emphasises that offensive operations are contemplated.

The document makes clear that Special Force Units were already being trained, and that these forces would be expanded in the future. It is not clear whether these differ from the Rangers element discussed above.

At point *'f.'*, referring to training of Officers to be geared to Northern Ireland, Captain Kelly has highlighted the second sentence recommending *"Closer Cooperation with nationalist organisations across the Border ... to provide the type of information envisaged"* and commented: *"Int Op.* [Operation]*"*—meaning that such work was assigned to the Intelligence Officers seconded to the North.

The document emphasises that the Government would have to specifically authorise Army training for deployment in the North.

Captain Kelly has noted against this paragraph *"Directive Foreseen"*. (He is talking about the Directive of 6th February, ordering the Army to be ready to make incursions into Northern Ireland. This appears Chapter Two.)

Point *'g.'*, *"Supporting the minority in the North by training and by supply of arms and equipment"*, is also highlighted by Captain Kelly, who comments on this section, which was germane to his duties as regards the North: *"Rifles Arms put up for sale later were obviously NOT part of these arms planned to be allotted to N.I. minority"*—meaning that the Army surplus rifles put up and then withdrawn from sale in 1969-70 were *not* the weapons it was planned to give to the minority—unless there was no other alternative in a sudden crisis. (They would have been traceable. That would not have mattered if the Army was openly deployed to the North, but would not have been appropriate if assistance to nationalists was to remain covert.)

Where the report suggests under point *g. (1)* that the numbers of Northerners wanting training would not be great, Captain Kelly notes, *"Doubtful comment"* and *"Int Report on B. Boro meeting to Government showed otherwise"*.

As for Point *g. (2)* on training nationalists, which he has highlighted, Kelly notes *"Training at Dunree"* and *"Training already started with Derrymen"*. (We will return to this matter in Chapter Three.)

Document 12: Council For Defence Meeting, 13 October

[I have found just one set of minutes of the Council for Defence in National Archive files, those for 13th October 1969. The meeting was called by Seán Ó Cearnaigh, the *Rúnaí*/Secretary at *An Roinn Cosanta*/Department of Defence with *Defence Policy* and *Vessels for the Naval Service* listed for the Agenda.

Strikingly, the Lynch loyalist, Desmond O'Malley TD, was one of the attendance of eight in his capacity as Parliamentary Secretary to the Minister for Defence. He was also Parliamentary Secretary to the Taoiseach and a regular attender at Cabinet. This combination of duties was of particular significance in the context of the Arms Crisis. After Taoiseach Lynch sacked Micháel O Morain on 5th May 1970, O'Malley became Minister for Justice, remaining in that position during the Arms Trials.]

"Meeting of the Council of Defence held on
13th October, 1969, in the Minister's Room, Parkgate

Present

James Gibbons, Minister for Defence, who presided.

Council of Defence.

Desmond O'Malley, T.D.
Parliamentary Secretary
to the Minister for Defence.
S. Ó Cearnaigh,
Secretary, Department of
Defence

Lt. General S. Mac Eoin,
Chief of Staff.
Colonel J. Emphy,
Adjutant-General.
Colonel W. Donagh,
Quartermaster-
General

Mr. P. Ó Cléirigh and Mr. P. Ó Murchadha, Assistant Secretaries, attended by permission of the Minister.

1. Vessels for the Naval Service.

The urgent necessity to provide vessels in order to maintain a fishery protection service was apparent. While naval type vessels were regarded as the appropriate medium, in the short term and as an emergency measure it might be necessary to use trawlers and certain enquiries in regard to such vessels were being made.

The Ghana frigate which had been offered for sale to the Department was a proposition which had some attractive features, notably the vessel was new, and immediately available and its reputed selling price was £2 1/2m. Its size, crew complement and cost of upkeep were aspects that might cause concern. However, it should be given serious consideration in the context of other possible solutions.

The Minister decided that the following steps should be taken:

(i) The efforts to locate suitable trawlers or other vessels in Britain and the Continent should continue.
(ii) Enquiries should also be made in U.S.A.
(iii) Further consideration should be given to the offer of the Ghana frigate.

These enquiries, which should proceed simultaneously, would be exploratory and without commitment. The urgency was such that representatives of the Department should call on possible suppliers if this would help to speed up matters.

In conjunction with the enquiries in U.S.A. about vessels, enquiries should also be made about the availability of military equipment generally as it was understood that the reduction of the U.S. war effort in Vietnam might release quantities of such equipment for disposal.

2. Defence Policy.

The Minister stated that there should be military plans for extreme contingencies arising from the situation in the North. The Chief of Staff pointed out that increased strength, adequate equipment, training, etc. such as advocated in the earlier studies on defence policy, were basic to any situation.

The question of intensive training of groups of personnel drawn from units of the Permanent Defence Force was discussed as was also the question of giving courses of continuous training, lasting some weeks, to elements of the F.C.A.

It was mentioned that these developments might give rise to public speculation and there might be local repercussions if barracks or posts were closed down to facilitate concentration of troops.

The serious lack of equipment and the inadequate financial provision for defence was adverted to.

The Minister decided that the Chief of Staff should submit a programme covering:

(a) intensive training of groups of personnel drawn from units of the Permanent Defence Force;
(b) special courses of continuous training for elements of the F.C.Á.;
(c) procurement of equipment.

This programme might be made the basis of an approach to the Government in regard to the securing of adequate financial provision.

3. Other Matters.

The Parliamentary Secretary suggested that officers of the Reserve 1st Line might be employed in F.C.Á. units instead of officers of the Permanent Defence Force. The Chief of Staff said that some consideration had already been given to this but there were considerable difficulties. It might be feasible in a few instances."

[NA 3-58367.]

Comment: These minutes are quite revealing, even though they have been composed with discretion. Though not minuted, it can be assumed that the troika reported to the Council on the recommendations of the Planning Board On Northern Ireland Operations. The minutes record Minister Gibbons instructing his Chief of Staff to submit a programme providing for intensive training of Army Units and special training for elements of the FCA.

The Army structure set up by Kevin Boland when he was Minister for Defence treated the FCA as an integral part of the Army, to be activated when the Army went into action. It is therefore understandable that extra training should now be envisaged.

But there is a second meaning to the decision to engage in training of *"elements"* of the FCA. Northerners were allowed to join this body if they gave Irish addresses. In this way Nationalist civilians in the Six Counties could be provided with military expertise. (I am informed that 'Northerners' could also join the Regular Army—for which 'Irish addresses' were not needed—and that many did so: many deserted in 1969-70, when trained, to return to the North.)

Paragraph *1. Vessels for the Naval Service* is ostensibly about obtaining a vessel for fishery protection. At the time there were certainly some foreign trawlers fishing in Irish waters. As they had to travel some distance, they tended to be bigger than the Irish vessels. But the idea that the Government might consider the use of *"trawlers"* for policing is puzzling. These tend to be slow boats, and speed would be a requirement for policing at sea.

Perhaps the suggestion in the last paragraph of item *1.*, that availability of American war surplus equipment should be investigated, may provide a pointer to Ministerial thinking. We have seen the Planning Board On Northern Ireland Operations suggest that British might cut off the Army stationed in Donegal, in which instance there would have to be supply by sea (Document 7, paragraph *8.*). A Quartermaster's report has also suggested that, in the event of hostilities, there might be difficulty in re-supply of weapons from abroad. There have also been several references to arming Northern nationalists in the above reports, something that could be done by sea. All in all, it is easy to see why acquiring a new vessel is treated with such urgency, and why *"trawlers"* might fit the bill.

Item 2 of the Agenda refers to *"extreme contingencies"*. Because of the foregoing reports, we have a good idea of the sort of thing this high-level military body had in mind. The points listed all have been dealt with in the preparatory reports we have seen. There is reference to the need to procure more equipment. The Quartermaster's 'shopping list' will be seen below.

There is no direct mention of Defence Regulation A.18 (which governs the military command structure), but it seems that it has been effectively over-ridden by the decision that the Chief of Staff should submit a programme, covering intensive training, special courses for *"elements of the F.C.A."*, and procurement of equipment, which could be taken to the Government.

The suggestion made by Desmond O'Malley under *Other Matters*, that Reserve Officers be used to train the FCA, is clearly intended to release regular officers for more active duties in this crisis.

A Council for Defence meeting must have been a rare occurrence: along with these minutes there is a note setting out the legal position of the Council, provision for which was made in the *Defence Act, 1954* (s.11). The legislation leaves the Minister free to issue invitations, and determine the agenda. The role of the Council is to "aid and counsel" the Minister.

As will be seen from these minutes, taken in the context of preceding documents, it is reasonable to conclude that Minister for Defence Gibbons and Parliamentary Secretary Desmond O'Malley were as closely implicated in arms 'smuggling' schemes as Charles Haughey—and that their activities in this field precede those of Captain Kelly. If arms had been imported for Northern nationalists in a naval vessel, Captain Kelly would not have been needed to organise the import of weapons. It would have been Gibbons and O'Malley who would have been 'smuggling' weapons for Northern nationalists.

Document 13: Preparations Continuing, 23 October

[Chief of Staff General Mac Eoin was instructed by Defence Minister Gibbons at the Council meeting recorded above to *"submit a programme"*, covering *"intensive training"* for regular troops; special courses for *"elements of the F.C.A."* (which included Northern civilians, as is established in a later chapter); and *"procurement of equipment"*. The Chief of Staff acted with alacrity. Below is the covering letter for the report which he submitted to the Minister on 23rd October:]

"

SCS 29

Br an Chinn Foirne,
CCA.

Aire Cosanta [Minister for Defence].

Uasail [Sir],

In accordance with your directions issued at the meeting of the Council of Defence on 13 Oct '69, I enclose paper outlining training and planning activity and the requirements of the Defence Forces in relation to arms, ammunition and equipment."

[SCS 18/1.]

Comment: I have not found the enclosure referred to above. But the covering letter makes it clear that the Army was still pursuing special military preparations as instructed.

Document 14: Rangers, FCA Training & Arms, 6 February 1970

[Four months after the Council for Defence meeting the Secretary to the Department of Defence sent the following memo to his Minister:]

" S/577

Aire

Defence Policy

...Arising out of events in the Six Counties, you directed at the Council of Defence meeting on 13/10/69 that a programme should be prepared covering certain training matters and the procurement of equipment. The statement dated 23/10/69 which was prepared by the military authorities sets out a programme of requirements in the matter of strengths, training, ammunition, arms and equipment. As part of a training programme ranger courses and group training have been in progress and personnel have been earmarked in the Commands to provide additional groups in the events of an emergency. Whereas the military authorities recommended increased training for the FCÁ at an estimated cost of £0.25 millions per year, you will recall that the Minister for Finance indicated to us recently that he would be prepared to sanction £50,000 for the purpose in the next financial year.

The statement of 23/10/1969 contains an estimate of £24.6 millions for ammunition, arms and equipment which represents an increase of £8. millions on the estimate for Army requirements in the Defence Policy Memorandum 1967. The increased figure is not incorporated in the draft Memorandum for the Government as the draft is confined to the position as presented in Defence Policy Memorandum 1967 and as decisions are not being sought at this stage on ammunition, arms and equipment.

S. Ó Cearnaigh
Rúnaí

6 Feabhra 1970"

[NA SCS 18/1.]

Comments: Secretary Ó Cearnaigh's memo is significant for a number of reasons, not least of which is the date: 6th February 1970 was the day that the Government took a decision to continue active military preparations for Northern military intervention in case of necessity. Afterwards the military command was called in and given instructions. A minute was made of that meeting, which appears in Chapter 2, *Government Directive Of 6th February 1970*.

By its date, the document above connects the Council for Defence meeting with the *Government Directive* of 6th February 1970.

Thus it is demonstrated that the *Government Directive* was part of a continuing policy of planning for active involvement in the North, which started after the August events, and which was confirmed by Minister Gibbons and Parliamentary Secretary O'Malley at the Council for Defence meeting of 13th October 1969.

Again, the document establishes that, six months after the events of August 1969, the Government was not winding down planning for military involvement in the North, but considered that nationalists remained in danger in the volatile situation.

It will be recalled that in Document 8 the Planning Board for Northern Ireland Operations called for the creation of special forces (23.d): we now find that *"ranger courses have been in training"*.

The Planning Board also called for special groups to start training for particular missions in the North (for instance *10.4.g*): this memo informs us that *"group training"* has commenced, with additional personnel *"earmarked"*.

The conclusion must be drawn that the Planning Board recommendations were not treated as a theoretical exercise, but were implemented at least in part.

As for Northern nationalists, that Board suggested that *Training* and *Arming* were the two easiest ways of assisting them. As we know, both were undertaken.

2. *Summary Of The Fourteen Documents*

In 46 years the Irish Army had never thought about 'invading' the North. The Government instruction in August 1969 that it should start thinking about that part of the United Kingdom in military terms was a shock. Nevertheless the Army considered what might be possible: military analyses and assessments were produced of how the Army could help the distressed minority. And reports were submitted showing what extra resources would be needed to implement such a task.

We have seen *Document One*, which speaks of *"rendering such assistance as may be desirable"* in Derry City and in which the Mission is *"explained verbally"* by the Chief of Staff.

Document Two discusses deploying an Army/Police presence in Coleman's Island using the element of surprise.

Document Three plans for regular war-gaming to be conducted in the Military College on a top-secret basis. The objective was *"intervention... to secure the safety of the minority population"* (*2.*). It suggests that preliminaries could be completed by May 1970.

The Quartermaster General comes into the picture with *Document Four*. His stock list of *Defensive Equipment* includes both offensive and defensive mortar and artillery ammunition, supplies for machine-guns and anti-aircraft guns, as well as a quarter of a million hand grenades and gas masks. He mentions the need to diversify supply.

In a further letter, *Document Five*, Col. MacDonnchadha/Donagh, Quartermaster

General, addresses the Contracts Officer about building up supplies and stresses the need to diversify sources from which armaments are obtained.

Document Six shows the Army purchasing extra munitions, along with other items enabling it to meet the demands of Government. Again diversification of suppliers is mentioned.

The attention of the Minister of Defence is directed to Army supply proposals in *Document Seven*. Cost implications of building up sufficient ammunition to service 8 days of conflict are raised. The reasons for stock-piling are frankly stated (British interference to prevent re-supply during any combat) as is the difficulty of engaging with unofficial arms dealers.

Document Eight is an Interim Report of the Planning Board on Northern Ireland Operations, which considers the type of assistance Irish military forces can give Northern Ireland nationalists in four types of situation they might be threatened by. The conclusion is that, while Irish Defence Forces have no capacity to engage in largescale operations against security forces in Northern Ireland, there is a capacity for conventional military operations up to the size of company level, and for unconventional operations if suitable preparations were made. The conventional operations could take place in areas near the Border, while unconventional operations would be appropriate for deeper objectives. Such deployments could entail cooperation with Civil Rights and Republican groups in the North, and possibly with illegal organisations in the South. These courses of action would require a seismic shift in the thinking of Irish Defence Forces from a defensive to an offensive orientation. If conventional operations are to proceed, an infantry battalion in each Command [that is, three Battalions] should be brought up to strength, trained and equipped to operate in company groups. The danger of British and Protestant extremist retaliation against the Republic should be considered. Training and Arming Northern nationalists would present no problem.

A second report from the Planning Board on Northern Ireland Operations, *Document Nine*, recommends setting up a special staff to prepare studies and plans *"for Border operations"*, which would prepare *"contingency operational plans"*.

Document Ten is the final report of the Planning Board for Northern Ireland Operations. The planning staff for the operations being considered should be capable of conducting them. Among the *"operations visualised"* are *"unconventional and support operations (supply and training)"*. The leadership of the three proposed full-strength Battalions should be introduced to the problem and given contingency missions.

Document Eleven is a commentary on the Planning Board's recommendations. This would rather see the existing seven Battalions brought up to full strength and armaments, rather than cannibalised to provide three Battalions capable of action. It raises the dangers for nationalists themselves, as well as for the Irish State, of open Irish military intervention. The extent of demand amongst Northern nationalists for weapons and training is questioned. It concludes that a requisite for military action is streamlining of command structures, extra military resources, and total commitment of the State.

Minister Jim Gibbons and Parliamentary Secretary Desmond O'Malley come into the picture with *Document Twelve*, the minutes of a Council of Defence meeting held to expedite military preparations. The Chief of Staff is instructed to prepare training programmes and shopping lists, whilst there is mention of buying a vessel for fishery protection and American surplus war equipment.

The cost implications of proposed arms purchases and extra FCA training are raised in *Document Thirteen.*

Four months after the Council for Defence meeting, *Document Fourteen*, a memo from Secretary Ó Cearnaigh to Minister Gibbons, shows that Chief of Staff Lt. General Sean Mac Eoin has put preparations in hand to implement the policy of giving military help to nationalists. He is implementing instructions to conduct training and has earmarked Army personnel to give extra assistance.

3. A Powerful Case

So, what do these fourteen documents amount to?

These official papers show that the Army responded with some urgency to the Cabinet instruction of mid-August 1969 to prepare to assist Northern nationalists.

The military thinking was that the Army could certainly assist the minority by providing arms and military training. Other missions were more problematical, given the relative strengths of the protagonists.

The essential point is that there was no squeamishness about guns in the official strategy of the Irish Government. The underlying message of these documents is that nationalists need, and are to get, military assistance of some sort. Spending priorities were to be amended accordingly.

There are warnings about providing overt help: nevertheless special training and planning initiatives are undertaken to prepare for this contingency. The incursions into Northern Ireland would be an act of war requiring appropriate weaponry to be acquired to cover contingencies. At the same time covert missions in the North are regarded as feasible.

The consistent message is that, while there are difficulties in openly confronting Northern Ireland security forces, there are few problems inherent in arming and training Northern nationalists to look after their own defence. Document *8.4.e.* refers to":

> "(1) Organising and conducting military training in the Republic for nationalists living in Northern Ireland.
> (2) Supplying arms, ammunition and equipment in accordance with availability to nationalist elements in Northern Ireland"

And this Report of the Planning Board for Northern Ireland Operations adds:

> "This type of action would involve relatively minor planning and training problems."

It goes on to say that:

> "the desirability of supporting the minority in the North by training and by the supply of arms and equipment [should] be considered, and if found to be acceptable, the development of plans for the implementation of these courses [should begin]" (*23.g.*)

The Board also suggested that *"the intelligence in the North be intensified and directed towards the courses of action suggested"* (*23.h.*).

All this provides a context for Captain Kelly's mission to assist Citizens' Defence in the North, and to provide liaison between the Defence Committees and the Government. As we know, he was one of up to a dozen Intelligence Officers assigned to provide assistance to the minority.

If the Army was going to arm nationalists covertly, it could not give them weapons from its own stockpiles, which would be traceable and bring retaliation on the Republic from the British State and Protestant extremists.

Initially, Northerners were subsidised by Government to purchase weapons but, when difficulties were experienced in the very substantial quantities of arms required, Captain Kelly was authorised to himself undertake arms-buying missions to the Continent.

It has been argued that Jack Lynch was either unaware of the military strategy of his Government in the months after August 1969, or that a couple of errant Cabinet Ministers acted on their own initiative and he did nothing to stop them.

These documents give the lie to such 'authoritative' statements by commentators with their own agendas.

The Army was implementing a policy of the Government, and that policy envisaged Training and Arming the Six-County Nationalists to defend their areas.

In the documents above there is no direct order from the Government to the Army to prepare to act. If such documents exist, they have not been released. Possibly such instructions were considered too delicate to be committed to paper. But that lacuna in our story is remedied on 6th February 1970.

Chapter Two

Government Directive To The Army

Frank Dunlop, the former head of the Government Press Office who became a star prosecution witness in the Tribunal investigating Planning Corruption after some irregularities in his own financial affairs were detected, has given an acute description of how Cabinet Government works in his *Yes, Taoiseach* (2004). It confirms what I had already discovered and alluded to in the first pamphlet in this series (*August 1969: Ireland's Only Appeal To The UN*). There I reproduced a Pink Minutes Slip, which in a byzantine way indicated the subject and date of a Cabinet meeting, but provided no further information (p80-1). Dunlop himself makes no mention of that procedure but, as an innovating Government press officer, he had to make sense of how the central apparatus of democracy worked. He was helped by senior civil servant Dan O'Sullivan—who was Secretary to the Taoiseach, to the Cabinet, and to the Government:

> "...When he sent me my first cabinet agenda I looked at it in amazement. It contained nothing more than requests for the government to authorize the publication of various Annual Reports of state and semi-state bodies and attached these huge wordy reports as addenda. There was nothing relating to government policy on anything, no matter how innocuous. When I brought this to his attention, he merely laughed and said that I would learn in due course that the more important matters were never put on the agenda and that in some instances the most important issues of all were never recorded" (p87)

It is possible that Dunlop is here confusing the meetings of the Government and those of the Cabinet. These are run consecutively, but are recorded in separate series of Minutes Books. The *Government* Minutes record mundane administrative decisions, while *Cabinet* minutes note at least some of the political decisions made. But in substance he is right: no delicate matters are committed to writing in the minutes of Cabinet meetings. Dunlop continues:

> "I did indeed learn that there was absolutely nothing on an agenda to indicate what might actually happen at a cabinet meeting. The items listed would be dealt with in a very short time, and it was then that the real business of government took place. And I was to learn in due course, as Dan O'Sullivan had said I would, that from time to time the Secretary to the Cabinet... left the cabinet meeting at the request of the Taoiseach and that the subsequent discussions, political or otherwise, were never recorded and therefore were never publicly acknowledged as ever having taken place. This was crucial to understanding how cabinet really worked..." (p88).

Of all the secret matters which Cabinet discussed down the years, how to respond to the plight of the Northern minority in 1969-70 was probably the most sensitive. That is why there are a host of blank Pink Slips in the released Cabinet Files for the first months of 1970, beginning with 10th February.

(Dunlop makes contradictory assertions about the Arms Crisis. On the one hand he concluded that, as a result of these customs, "it is doubtful that we will ever know the truth of what actually happened" (p88); that senior Fianna Fail figures told him "the government as a whole knew that 'certain actions' were being taken to try to alleviate the situation for the Nationalist community in the North"; and that there were "some difficult questions as to the extent of Jack's and the Cabinet's knowledge about what Charlie and others were allegedly up to" (p225). On the other, he speaks of "the disclosure [in 1970] that there had been an attempt to import arms illegally" (p9); and refers to—

> "The generally accepted political view… that there was an attempt to import arms illegally, that Charlie was involved and that in court he preferred to deny it" (p15).

The crucial word in these remarks is *illegal*. There can be no doubt that there was an attempted importation of arms. No one at the Arms Trials denied it—not Charles Haughey and certainly not Captain Kelly who insisted on it. But, if the importation was authorised by the Government, it was *legal* in Irish law. The jury in the October 1970 Arms Trial was fully convinced, on the basis of hearing the evidence, that Government had approved the importation of arms, and therefore it took hardly any time to return a Not Guilty verdict on the four defendants (Captain Kelly, Charles Haughey, John Kelly, and Albert Luykx). Dunlop seems not to have absorbed that fact, though he attended the Trials (while a student).

To describe the attempted importation as *illegal* is to adopt the standpoint of an alien juridical system which had no legal force within Ireland. The attempted importation of arms for Northern nationalist defence was quite legal in the Irish jurisdiction as it was authorised by government. But it was an affront to British authority and, whatever about the statutes, sufficient law would have been found to prosecute the principals in Britain if that was considered to be in the British interest. It was *illegal* only in British terms.)

No minute exists of a Cabinet decision to order military assistance to Northern nationalists. But what is missing from Government records is provided by the body to which that instruction was given, the Army Command. The Cabinet was careful about what it committed to paper. The Army could not afford to be as cautious. The serious nature of the orders it received required them to be committed to paper, albeit to be revealed only to a very small circle. This was an essential mechanism to prevent later recrimination or criminalisation, but only the leading officers gave themselves this protection. Captain Kelly was given only verbal instructions. And, when he later tried to obtain 'Discovery' of the relevant

Government Directive for his legal defence case in September 1970, the Court was told by the Army authorities that the document was lost.

Fortunately for James Kelly, however, there was one straightforward and brave man in the Army Command, his immediate superior, the Director of Military Intelligence.

One of the things which helped to convince the Arms Trial jury of the legitimacy of the attempted importation of arms was Colonel Michael Hefferon's testimony about the Government Directive. He recalled its main points from memory and from notes he made at the time. The jury found his evidence compelling.

Rather surprisingly, Army Minutes of that Ministerial Directive have now been released to the public. They are reproduced below.

There are other documents, too, which sustain the case that this is no single aberrant order pertaining to a momentary crisis, but a consistent military strategy in keeping with the new departure described in the last Chapter.

We have seen that the highest circles of the Irish Defence establishment were aware of, and involved in, planning for Northern Ireland operations from mid-August 1969 onwards. Nevertheless, there is a note of surprise—not to say reluctance—implicit in the reactions of the few officers made privy to the Government Directive of 6th February 1970. So much so that General Mac Eoin asked to address the Cabinet; and a list of questions was drawn up for Minister Gibbons to answer.

Then there are documents which show Chief of Staff General Mac Eoin working out the practical implications of Government military strategy.

To round out the collection, there are Colonel Delaney's observations on why these Government plans should never be revealed.

Taken together, the released *Secret* material reproduced below shows that the military preparations outlined in Chapter One did indeed form part of a consistent Government strategy which continued well into 1970. Captain Kelly's liaison work with Northern defence groups fed back into this strategy. And his buying of weapons on the Continent formed an essential element in it.

1. Documents, 1970

Document 15: Government Directive To Army, 6 February

[On 6th February the Cabinet held a meeting on the Northern Ireland crisis. External Affairs Minister Patrick Hillery submitted a paper for consideration. He also submitted a separate *Note For The Taoiseach*, in which he explained that his memorandum assumed that "a genuine attempt was being made, under direct UK supervision, to establish equality of treatment for all in the affairs of the Six Counties and that relative calm will result when this policy is seen to be effective". He went on to set out five scenarios, should this assumption prove to be incorrect. The fifth of these was as follows:

> "*Alternative V* It is necessary to consider the possibility that the North will fall apart in the near future and that widespread disorder will occur through the Six Counties which will be incapable of being contained by the British Army. There would be a grave risk of cross-Border incursions but the initial reactions of the Government should be political and every effort made, while circumstances permit it, to avoid unilateral military involvement. Ultimately this alternative is covered by the Taoiseach's statement of August 13th - "that the Irish Government can no longer stand by and see innocent people injured and perhaps worse"."

[NA 2000/6/513.]

A Cryptic record of that Government meeting was made by the Cabinet Secretary on a Pink Slip (which is reproduced on page 69):

> "6 Feabhra 1970
>
> ...
>
> *Northern Ireland Policy*
>
> P
>
> {informally agreed that
>
> (1) sale of arms surplus to Army requirements, for which tenders were recently invited, should not now take place.
>
> (2) Minister for Finance, in consultation with Minister for Defence, would see how far he could go towards meeting cost of essential items of military vehicles & other equipment included in a recent application from Department of Defence for sanction of £13 m. for this purpose &
>
> (3) Taoiseach, in consultation with Minister for External Affairs, would consider nature of an approach to British Government to inquire what they propose to do to meet present worsening situation in Six Counties.}"

[NA 2001/6/513.]

Chief of Staff Mac Eoin was called in after that meeting, and we learn from Army minutes that the decisions reached at that Cabinet meeting were more far-reaching than indicated above:]

CRUINNIÚ RIALTAIS

6 Feabhra 1970

~~Rialt.~~/Comh-Air. Uimh. 1

Northern Ireland: Policy

An Bhreith :

[Informally agreed that

(1) sale of arms surplus to Army requirements, for which tenders were recently invited, should not now take place,

(2) Minister for Finance, in consultation with Minister for Defence, would see how far he could go towards meeting cost of essential items of military vehicles & other equipment included in a recent application from Department of Defence for sanction of £13 m. for this purpose &

(3) Taoiseach, in consultation with Minister for External Affairs, would consider nature of an approach to British Government to inquire what they propose to do to meet present worsening situation in Six Counties.]

(6858)M27145. 5,000. 12-67. F.P.—G28.

Pink Slip recording Cabinet Meeting of 6th February 1970

"TOP SECRET

STRN [Director of Training] Copy No FIVE

RN P & O [Planning & Operations Section]
CCA [Army HQ]
10/2/70

Ministerial Directive
to Chief of Staff
16.30 hrs Friday
6 Feb. 70

1. Present when conveyed by CF 1700 hrs 6 Feb. AG, ACS, S Faios, Lt Col Adams.

2. Directive

a. "to prepare and train the Army for incursions into Northern Ireland."
b. Respirators ?
c. Weapons and arms, surplus ?
d. The exact nature of the directive in regard to b and c was NOT mentioned by CF
e. The following questions arise out of a.
(1) the probable purpose of such incursions
(2) when and in what circumstances
(3) are ops to be "large" scale or of a small hit and run nature
(4) are incursions to be overt or covert
(5) limitations or stipulations as to number of pers to be involved
(6) are ops to be with or without prejudice to all other tasks such as the security of posts and the protection of vital instls

3. Implications

In view of the possible implications of the directive, it would seem essential that the Minister and the Cabinet would make arrangements to hear the CF on these aspects at 2 e above and on the critical state of the Army to undertake such a mission

4. Suggested planning procedure

a. Meeting — CF and S Fais to get in writing the exact nature of the directive
b. Staff Conference — CF, AG ACS QMG or Deputy SP&O S Fais S Im
(1) Discussion of mission
(2) Determination of planning sequence
(3) Types of forces to be used, Comd commitments - type of ops.
(4) Training
(5) Control of ops - comns
(6) Level to which planning will go
(7) Cover plan
(8) Special Planning staff

c. Command OCs meeting
To attend Comd OCs, S cori, Staff as at 4a above
Broad plan / Comd commitments
Cover plan

5. Respirators, Surplus arms and amn.

Distr a Q problem

a. How many

b. Where to be held

c. How to be packed

d. To whom to be delivered

e. Stand by transport

f. Officer i/c.

J.A."

[NA MDA.]

Comments: This is one of the most crucial Arms Crisis documents to be released into the public domain. It is a record of a Government Directive given to the Chief of Staff by the Minister for Defence, and makes clear that the Cabinet decided to order the Army to prepare for direct intervention in Northern Ireland. Point *3.* makes clear that the orders here recorded come from Cabinet and not just from Minister Gibbons.

In the last Chapter we saw the Army planning, training, and making other preparations to assist the Northern minority. But we had to deduce that the military had been ordered to act on these lines. Now we have evidence of formal orders that were so far-reaching in their implications that the Army Command felt obliged to commit them to paper, at least in part. One of the Orders was that the Army was to *"prepare for incursions into Northern Ireland"*.

Although these minutes do not mention it, Col. Hefferon was already in James Gibbons' office when Lt. General Mac Eoin arrived to receive his instructions, and they were passed on in his presence.

The Director of Intelligence had been in close communication with the Minister for Defence over Northern military initiatives from mid-August 1969 onwards. And the minutes above show that he continued to play a crucial role. He is listed above as attending this meeting (*S. Fais*). And he is amongst those called to two further conferences to consider how the orders should be implemented: an initial Staff Conference (*4.b.*) and a wider meeting of Commanders in the field (*4.c.*). Significantly, he is delegated (*4.a.* above) to approach the Government with Chief of Staff Mac Eoin and get the Government Directive in writing. All this confirms what we know from other sources: that Colonel Hefferon was a key player in the Government's new military departure. To have such an officer giving evidence which exonerated the defendants in the Arms Trials undermined the prosecution case and makes it hard to understand why Taoiseach Lynch decided to bring a criminal prosecution against Cabinet colleagues who had taken part in formulating the new military policy and an Army Captain who was putting it into effect.

The command received the instructions in the Government Directive with some discomfort: which is why it was agreed that Mac Eoin should seek to address the Cabinet (point *3.*). (This would not have been the first time he attended Cabinet: he was called in for consultation at an emergency meeting in mid-August 1969.)

One problem was that the military was already stretched in meeting its commitments. Its best units were on UN duties and, since the UVF attack on Ballyshannon Power Station in October 1969, the guarding of vital installations had taken on a new importance. While it was true that the Army was ill-prepared and inadequately-equipped for military action, there must be a suspicion that the fear of putting themselves 'in the wrong', in United Nations terms, with incursions into the territory of a friendly State, is also an underlying factor. Foreign reactions are certainly adduced by the incoming Director of Army Intelligence, Colonel Delaney, for suppressing the truth of what happened after the event (see Document 30).

The implications of Point *2.a.* above (order to prepare to mount incursions) are teased out in *2.e.* The sort of questions that are asked indicate a familiarity with the kind of operations mapped out by the Planning Board On Northern Ireland Operations, which we saw in the last Chapter (Document 8). There, a lot of different options were sketched out, under a number of scenarios. For instance—

> " 6. Situation B [Catholics v. NI Security Forces]
> a. To conduct conventional operations up to coy level directly at Northern Ireland Security Forces.
> b. In conjunction with 'a' above, conventional operations up to coy level directed at key areas along the Border designed to draw Security Forces away from the area of direct conflict.
> c. A wide range of unconventional operations in any part of Northern Ireland designed to draw forces off from the area of direct conflict independently or in conjunction with a. and b. above."

Thus we have the meeting of 6th of February asking for clarification as to *"when and in what circumstances"* (*2.e.(2)*) the Army is to be deployed. In Document 8 four possible such scenarios were teased out.

Again, it was asked whether operations were to be large- or small-scale. Document 8 had emphasised that small interventions were more feasible and less risky

It was questioned whether intervention was to be *"overt or covert"* (*2.e.(4)*). Document 8 suggested operations to defend Catholics where they formed the minority would have to be covert (e.g. point *19*), while overt operations could be mounted in areas near the Border.

A curious question that was asked on 6th February was: what the *"cover plan"* would be. In fact, the question is raised twice (*4.b.(7)* and *4.c.*). As we know, in mid-August 1969 the pretext for troop movements and mobilisations was the 'humanitarian' need to establish field hospitals and refugee camps. Now there was going to be a need to hide the true significance of further special preparations, in order to maintain the element of surprise.

The suggestion that a *"cover plan"* was needed suggests an Army belief that it was being asked to mount more than minor operations in the North.

One aspect of the Cabinet orders transmitted by Minister Gibbons on 6th February 1970 remains implicit: it is not recorded as such in these minutes. These do not say in so many words that the Cabinet ordered the Army to arm the Northern minority. Nevertheless, a careful reading of the minutes reveals that Mac Eoin was ordered to make preparations for this eventuality and that he told his fellow Army commanders of this order. That is clear from points *2.b.,c.,d.* and from point *5.* No other meaning can be drawn from the words recorded.

It will be recalled that the fourth option listed in Point 6 of Document 8 (Planning Board for Northern Ireland Operations) was—

> "d. In conjunction with a. and b. and c. above, the supply of arms, ammunition, equipment and medical supplies to Catholic minority, in accordance with availability."

Point *2.c.* speaks in particular of *"Weapons and arms, surplus"*. From other sources we know that it is referring to Army surplus weaponry which was not sold off but kept back for possible defensive use by Northern Nationalists. As we shall see, there was a scare in early April when the weapons were rushed North to Dundalk in readiness for distribution.

The reference to *"respirators"* bears out this analysis. As we saw in Chapter 1, the Army requested purchase of 10,000 respirators (Document 4, *7.d.*). This is far more than would have been needed for the Army's own use. We will see that respirators were part of the consignment rushed to Dundalk a couple of months later.

Significantly, point *2.d.* indicates that *"the exact nature of the directive in regard to b and c was NOT mentioned by CF"*. In other words, Mac Eoin did not specify what material was to be distributed or to whom. The assumption is made in this point that it is surplus arms that will be distributed and questions are drawn up to clarify recipients and mode of transfer. This paragraph is another firm indication that we are not talking about weapons being moved around within the Army. The Army command would hardly be likely to be asking for Ministerial clarification about where to hold its own armoury! There can be no other meaning to points *a.* to *f.* but that the Army has been ordered to prepare to give weapons to Northern Nationalists.

The commanders present ask *"to whom to be delivered?"* (*5.d*). As we shall see, when it appeared that the arms were going to be handed out in a hurry, a message was sent to Captain Kelly, the Government's liaison officer with the Northern defence groups and the only person in the whole Army with a comprehensive knowledge of who weapons should be given to. Captain Kelly was on the Continent, arranging for arms shipments, at the time.

The Army personnel implicated in this *Top Secret* meeting were:

Chief of Staff Mac Eoin (CF/Chief of Staff);
Col. J. Emphy (AG/Adjutant General);
Col. W.H. Byrne (ACS/Assistant Chief of Staff);
Col. Hefferon (S. Faois/Director of Intelligence); and
Lt. Col. Adams (Rng P70/Planning & Operations Section at Army HQ).

The document originates in the Planning & Operations Sections, at Army HQ (RN P & O, CCA).

The copy we have is addressed to *STRN*, who I take to be the Director of Training, Daniel Fitzgerald. He receives *"Copy No FIVE"*.

It was proposed to involve, additionally:

Col. William Donagh/Cornal L. MacDonnchadha (QMG /Quartermaster General) or his Deputy;
Col. S.C. Ó Donnabháin/O'Donovan (SP&O/Director, Planning & Operations);
S Im: this could be the Director of Supply and Transport (*Iompair*);
Command OCs; (these were: Eastern Command (possibly Col. J.H. Byrne); Col. C. O'Sullivan (Southern); Col. C.E. Shortall (Western); and Col. J.J. Quinn (Curragh)); and
S CORI (who is probably the Director of the Corps of Engineers).

Document 16: Addendum To Government Directive of 6 February

[Although Minister Gibbons issued the Government Directive on 6th February 1970, the minutes above are dated 10th February.

The sequence of events appears to have been as follows. The Cabinet met on 6th February 1970. In consequence Minister Gibbons gave a verbal Ministerial Directive to his Army Chief of Staff at 2.30 on the same day in the presence of the Army Director of Intelligence, Colonel Hefferon. And General Mac Eoin passed the orders on to four senior officers at 4.30pm. They advised that Ministerial orders be clarified and obtained in writing.

A Cabinet meeting was held on 10th February, for which we have a blank Pink Slip, indicating that the contents were too sensitive to record even in a cryptic manner. (It is reproduced on page 75.)

It may or may not be a coincidence that the minutes of the Government Directive were set down on the same day as the Cabinet held a second ultra-private meeting.

CRUINNIÚ RIALTAIS

10 Feabhra 1970

~~Rialt.~~/Comh-Air. Uimh. 2

Northern Ireland: Policy.

An Bhreith :

P

(6858)M27145. 5,000. 12-67. F.P.—G28.

Pink Slip recording a Cabinet Meeting on 10th February 1970

On the next day, 11th February, the Chief of Staff included a further officer in the secret, Col. S.C. Ó Donnabháin/O'Donovan who held the post of Director, Planning and Operations (S/P&I). Lt. Col. J. Adams again took the minutes, which are important because they run over, and give further details of, the *Ministerial Directive* of 6th February.

The *"Memo of 10/2/70"* in the title below are the minutes above.

It will be noted that the two paragraphs, at *1. a.* and *b.*, have inverted commas in the original, meaning they are a direct quotation of Minister Gibbons' words on 6th February. The *"I"* is Minister Gibbons, and the *"you"* is General Mac Eoin. *CF* is the Chief of Staff. And again the minutes have *Top Secret* stamped and written on them:]

"TOP SECRET

S Im

Copy No 5
Rn P & O
CCA
11/2/70

Addendum to Memo of 10/2/70
Ministerial directive
to CF

Present CF, S/P&I, Lt Col Adams.

1. At a meeting held on 11/2/70, CF recapitulated on Ministers directive as follows.

a. "At a meeting of the Government held this morning (Friday 6 Feb 70) I was instructed to direct you to prepare the Army for incursions into Northern Ireland."

b. "The Taoiseach and other Ministers have met delegations from the North. At these meetings urgent demands were made for respirators, weapons and ammunition the provision of which the Government agreed. Accordingly truck loads of these items will be put at readiness so that they may be available in a matter of hours.["]

c. Minister asked what were the natures of critical deficiencies to which CF answered

Manpower
AFVs [Armoured Fighting Vehicles]
TPT [Transport]

d. The Minister directed that the FCA should be required to take on more security tasks than at present in order to free PDF [Permanent Defence Force] pers for training and ops.

e. The Minister instructed CF to hold himself in readiness to discuss estimates with Mr Haughey as soon as the latter was out of hospital.

J.A."

[NA MDA.]

Comments: We have here a *reprise* of the Government instructions in Document 15. But this time there is more detail. It is as if the Chief of Staff has seen the Minister in between and obtained permission to be more frank with other commanders. In the first minutes (Document 15) it is said *"The exact nature of the directive"* was not conveyed, but that is remedied above.

Thus the second minutes clarify some of the questions raised at the first. For instance, in the first minutes, it was asked who weapons were to be given to, how they were to be *"packed"*, and what *"standby transport"* there was to be. Here we are told frankly that *"truck loads"* will be placed *"in readiness"*, and that the weapons are to meet requests made to Government Ministers by delegations from the North. (It goes without saying that these were from the Nationalist community.) These groups were of mixed composition: those seeking these means of defending their communities included elected politicians, community activists, and members of the IRA.

The deductions we were able to make from the minutes of 10th February are confirmed explicitly on the 11th.

This copy *"No 5"*, again originating from the Planning & Operations Section at Army HQ is addressed to S Im (possibly the Director of Supply & Transport).

But what jumps out and bites you from this *Top Secret* document is Gibbons informing the Army that ***"the Government agreed"*** to supply Northerners with *"respirators, weapons and ammunition"*, at the request of delegations from the North.

Significantly, ***the Taoiseach is specifically mentioned*** by the Minister for Defence as being involved—even though, just a couple of weeks earlier, Jack Lynch made a vigorous speech to the Fianna Fail Ard Fheis, declaring that conquest of the North was neither feasible nor desirable, which was generally taken as a put-down of republican elements in the Party and confirming a policy of quiescence.

Compare this *Addendum* with the following evidence, given by Minister Gibbons at the first Arms Trial. He is being questioned by John Kelly's counsel, Seamus Sorohan, about a long meeting the Minister had with a Northern Defence delegation in early March 1970:

> "Mr. Sorohan: The question of arms was discussed for an appreciable time
>
> Mr. Gibbons: Yes. One of the things I can recall being discussed was the dire situation of certain people in the city of Belfast whose houses had been surrounded by Saracen armoured cars and British troops in order to protect them from fanatics of one kind and another.
>
> Mr. Gibbons said that the discussion, and it had been confirmed by intelligence, had suggested a future in that area of a very ominous nature. The future estimation of what would happen in this area before the year was over was very grim indeed.
>
> Mr. Sorohan: You did not promise them that they would get arms?
>
> Mr. Gibbons: No" (Irish Times, 25.9.70, p11).

Colonel Hefferon also gave evidence about the Government Directive. He said—

"...he was aware of a directive issued to the Army and had discussed with Captain Kelly that implications of that directive..." [IT 29.9.1970, p8, c8.]

"Mr. McKenna: ...can you recall from whom came the first mention of the Government?

Colonel Hefferon: This is difficult to say. From February 6th or so when this directive was issued which indicated a firmer attitude towards the planning, I had many conversations with Captain Kelly in which he kept me informed about the activities of delegations coming down from Northern Ireland that the Minister may have met...

...all these people looked for arms and ammunition and gas masks; these were the main requisitions they made; and ... in conversation with various Government Ministers they had been promised help in this matter..." [Ibid, p9, c3.]

"Mr. Finlay [barrister for Captain Kelly]: A general directive was given to the Army I think on February 6th by the Minister for Defence, Mr. Gibbons?

Colonel Hefferon: Yes... The directive was to the Chief of Staff. The general terms were that surplus arms and ammunition would be set aside and made available for such contingencies.

Mr. Finlay: Did you discuss that directive with Captain Kelly?

Colonel Hefferon: I did, about a week after the directive was issued.

Colonel Hefferon told Mr. Justice O'Keeffe that the directive was that the Army was to prepare for incursions into Northern Ireland and set aside surplus arms and ammunition and plan for these incursions and that they were to provide also gas masks...

Mr. Finlay: Did that discussion include a discussion on the possible contingency of having to distribute arms to the civilian population?

Colonel Hefferon: Yes that arises from the directive...

Mr. Finlay: Was one of the matters you discussed that if such a contingency did arise that it would be very desirable if the arms were untraceable?Colonel Hefferon: I don't recall discussing that with him at this time, but way back in September or October we had gone into this question in some detail..."

(Ibid, p9, c5.)

It is clear from these quotations, in the context of the documents above, that Colonel Hefferon was telling the truth at the Arms Trial and Minister Gibbons was not.

Colonel Delaney, Hefferon's successor, prepared a *Secret* damage-limitation commentary after Hefferon gave his evidence. Here he attempts to rebut the *"allegation"* of *"Colonel HEFFERON and Captain KELLY that the Directive was a "back-up" for the purchase of Pistols"* (see Document 30). But the jury found otherwise.

After conveying the Directive to General Mac Eoin, the Minister for Defence instructed the commander "to hold himself in readiness to discuss estimates with Mr Haughey on his release from hospital" (NA S 650, see Document 26 below. I have not been able to confirm how long Haughey was in Hospital for at this time).

Document 17: Army Questions To Minister, 17 February

[Moving very quickly, the Army conducted a military study of the Government Directive, identified questions to be answered, and obtained a meeting with Minister Gibbons on 13th February 1970. The following account of the questions asked and answers received was drawn up by the Army:]

" (1) The Military assume that incursions would only be mounted in circumstances where there would be a complete break-down of law and Order in N. Ireland and where the Security Forces were unable or unwilling to protect the Minority	The Minister confirmed that such a situation was what was envisaged
(2) The Military assume that the sole object of incursions would be the protection of the lives and property of the minority	The Minister confirmed that such was envisaged
(3) The military requested information regarding the Government's intention to make diplomatic representations before incursions	The Minister did not consider that such representations would be made
(4) The Chief of Staff queried if the Government intended in the circumstances of incursions, (a) to declare a state of emergency (b) to introduce the National Security Bill (c) to introduce a form of compulsory military service	The Minister thought that the Government would declare a state of emergency
(5) In view of the absolute necessity to ensure secrecy in contingency planning, the Chief of Staff enquired how much information had been given to the Northern delegations of the Government's intentions	The Minister indicated that the Northern delegations had not been informed of the directive to the Defence Forces.
(6) In view of the critical shortage of armoured cars, can the Panhards be withdrawn from Cyprus	The Government does not approve of their withdrawal
(7) In view of critical shortages of	A Council of Defence Meeting

of AFV, will the Government approve a Purchase mission to the United States	would be necessary to determine priorities
(8) In view of the nature of the directive can the financial restrictions on the employment of FCA be eased to provide for greater FCA participation and the consequent release of PDF personnel for urgently needed training	This would have to be examined in detail.
(9) Can the overall limitation on the permitted strength of the PDF be lifted in view of the directive	Estimates provide for 7500 but Minister for Finance is likely to sanction an increase
(10) Can the present strength on border posts be reduced in view of the heavy commitments on vital installations and the need to release men for training	Approved
(11) Has the Secretary of the Department been informed of the nature of the directive	Yes
(12) With regard to the arms, ammunition and respirators (a) How many are to be made available (b) To whom and in what circumstances are they to be handed over	The Minister had no idea but agreed that stockpiles were to be held in Dublin and Athlone "

[NA S 650, see Document 24 below, where this forms paragraph e.]

Comments: The point of the first two questions from the military is to establish that the Government is not contemplating force to bring about a United Ireland. That is why Question (2) speaks of the *"sole object"* of the incursion. The Minister confirmed that the Government did not envisage any wider object.

With these questions the Army established that incursions into Northern Ireland were to be of limited extent, to protect the lives and property of the *"Minority"* in the context of a *"State of Emergency"*. At first I read the Government Directive as issuing orders to prepare for 'rescue missions', *"incursions"* to escort nationalists under attack into safety across the Border. But, studying the other documents, it was borne in on me that, while that is one aspect covered by the Cabinet orders, the task set was much wider.

Protecting *"property"* (point 2 above) suggests a continuing presence. How else, for instance, could you prevent houses being burnt down? It seems clear to me that the Government Directive allows for area defence in minority areas—

which was to be as extensive as location and resources permitted. It also allows for all sorts of operations to be mounted if lives and property were in serious danger.

As we saw in the last Chapter, the Planning Board On Northern Ireland Operations indicated that the Army might mount mobile missions in areas away from the Border, but be in a better position to assist defence in areas near the Border (Document 8). And the questions drawn up by the high command (Document 15) were clearly framed in the context of the Planning Board's thinking.

Significantly the Minister for Defence indicated that Britain would not be given prior notice. As we shall see in Document 30, that rankled with elements of the Army command.

As for robbing the Irish United Nations contingent of their armoured cars, it is not surprising that this was rejected out of hand. The Cabinet had in August 1969 rejected Kevin Boland's proposal to bring home these Irish troops, despite his resignation (subsequently withdrawn). At the same time, the failure to withdraw from UN commitments in this Irish military emergency confirms the lack of seriousness in Cabinet responses identified in the first pamphlet in this series.

The Planning Board On Northern Ireland Operations saw *arming* and *training* as two things which might easily be done across the board. And it would have been Catholic enclaves in places like Belfast which would have been most in need of this kind of help. The Directive of 6th February gave legs to that recommendation, but James Gibbons refused to be drawn by the Army's questioning about the quantities of weapons to be set aside for the Nationalist minority—which was not surprising as a substantial second line of supply was currently being arranged.

The Army was here clarifying both aspects of the Government Directive of 6th February: both the military incursions and the supply of weapons to Northern nationalists. The juxtaposition of the two instructions might suggest that weapons were only to be distributed to Nationalists in conjunction with Army incursions. But that there was no intrinsic link between these two aspects of Cabinet military policy is shown by Document 21 below. Weapons could be provided to Nationalists whether there were incursions or not.

Document 18: Army Weapons For The Minority, February

[The following is a list of the Army weapons set aside for distribution to the Northern minority in the first instance on foot of the Directive of 6th February:]

"On 18 Feb 1970, the following items were assembled in Dublin and Athlone

Each	500	Rifles No 4
	200	Gustav MGs [machine guns]
	3000	Respirators
	80,000	rounds 303 amn
	99,000	rounds 9 mm amn. "

[NA S 650, see Document 24 below, of which this forms part; also see NA MI4. The equipment for the North was kept on trucks, which were standing by in case of sudden need.]

Comments: Again, we find the Army acting rapidly on foot of the Directive, with substantial arrangements in place in under two weeks.

The large quantities set aside may seem surprising, but it should be remembered that Northern Ireland Catholics had virtually no weapons at this time. Cathal Goulding had withdrawn IRA weaponry from the North and reportedly sold a substantial part of his arsenal to the Free Wales Army. On the other side, there were heavily-armed official security forces, not fully under Government control. And private unionist military organisations were importing further arsenals. The British Army was not deployed in sufficient quantities to guarantee the safety of all Catholic areas.

The quantities listed are broadly comparable to those which Captain Kelly was arranging to import, except that he was charged with attempting to import 500 Luger pistols with 80,000 rounds of ammunition, rather than rifles.

Document 19: Army Requirements, 27 February

[As a result of the Government decision of 6th February, External Affairs Minister Hillery had a formal meeting on 20th February with a British delegation headed by Minister George Thomson at which he pressed the British side about the drift to the right in Unionism, and about long-term reform plans. That same day a report to the Irish Government noted that: "The UVF continued their series of explosions during the week" (NA 2001/6/513).

Speaking of "the accumulation of weapons in private hands", Hillery told Thomson "he was concerned at the prospect of Protestant extremists becoming more aggressive once again, under the protection of the British Army" (NA; D/T, Partition. Govt Policy, 29.12.69-23.4.70).

The Irish Cabinet held another secret meeting on 24th February, for which there is a blank Pink Slip in the file (not reproduced here). It must be concluded that the Government was not satisfied with the British response, as it proceeded with its own military preparations.

In his June 1970 report for Taoiseach Lynch (Document 24 below), General Mac Eoin says he "formed a small selected planning Board to implement the Government's directive" (NA S650, see Document 24 below). But we do not have the terms of reference given to this Planning Board. Here is a report which was submitted to the Minister for Defence within three weeks of the Directive. The essential message is that shortage of resources has compromised military capacity:]

"SECRET

SCS 29
Oifig an Chinn Fóirne,
CCA.
27/2/1970.

Aire Cosanta.

Military Preparedness

Uasail,

Since 1962 the following papers prepared by the military side for submission to the Government have stressed the grave weaknesses in the capabilities and preparedness of the Defence Forces, and in particular the Permanent Defence Forces element to meet a situation of war or other urgent demands, even of a limited nature[,] which may be made by the Government.

Ireland in a Major War	Oct 1962
Memorandum on Defence Policy	July 1963
Defence Review Board Report	1965
Defence Policy Memorandum	1967

Events since 13 Aug 1969, necessitating the deployment of forces in the Border area and in the protection of important installations, have only served to reinforce the views expressed in these papers.

In anticipation of possible demands on the Government for active military assistance in the N.I. situation the following papers have been submitted since Aug 1969.

Preparedness of the Defence Forces	25 Aug 69
Estimate of the situation	6 Sept 69
SCS 19/1, Requirements of Defence Forces	23 Oct 69 (Copy attached [not reproduced here])

As I am not aware whether any or all of these papers have been submitted to the Government, I am concerned lest the Government may not be fully informed regarding the ill-preparedness of the Defence Forces to implement the direction conveyed by An tAire [Minister Gibbons] on 6 Feb 1970.

The ill-preparedness of the Permanent Defence Forces, which is the only element immediately available at all times, stems from shortages in manpower and essential operational equipment.

Strength

The present strength of the Permanent Defence Force at 8,416 shows an overall deficiency of 4,655 (34%) against establishments. The strength of NCOs and Privates at 7,331 shows a deficiency of 4,355 (38%). Even by taking into account the 400 odd First Line Reservists still on permanent service, the deficiency is 32%. The greatest part of these deficiencies occurs in the junior ranks which are normally made up of the younger age groups; in fact we are short a total of 300 junior officers; 500 corporals and 3,600 privates. It is the military view that the strength required to carry out the Government directions of 6 Feb 70 would be about 15,000, made up of some 1,400 officers and 13,600 men. In these circumstances the proposal of An Rúnaí to limit the strength of NCOs and privates to 7,100 plus 450 recruits is considered unrealistic.

Effects of low Strength

After making allowance for non-combat units such as the Air Corps, Naval Service, Medical Service, Recruits, Apprentices, Band Boys, Administrative, Garrison and training establishments and the high proportion of all ranks unfit for arduous combat duties for age and medical reasons, the total number available for the combat units of the Infantry, Cavalry and Artillery Corps is not much in excess of 2,000.

The net effect is that not one unit is combat effective within its own resources and it was found necessary to draw on administrative and training units and cadres to make up the improvised groups deployed since Aug 1969.

Even these limited deployments have so stretched the available manpower that the heavy incidence of duties is causing concern from the point of view of morale and is seriously hampering the training necessary to implement the recent Government direction.

Employment of the Reserve

While it is the military opinion that an overall strength of about 15,000 would be required in the new situation and is the figure to be aimed at, it is realised that such a strength in trained men could not be attained in the immediate future. In these circumstances the only alternative as a short term emergency solution is to call out part of the Reserve to complete establishments of field units. A contingency plan, "First Step", designed to meet the requirements of the Government direction provides for the calling out of the full First Line Reserve and selected members of the FCA. An outline of this plan showing the sources of supply is attached. This, however, can only be regarded as an interim step prior to the full mobilisation of the Defence Forces.

As the many problems likely to arise from a decision to call out part of the FCA will need careful preparations an early indication of policy in that regard is essential.

Estimates 1970/71

The Military proposals for Defence purchases on which the present estimates are based were submitted in July 1969 and therefore did not take into account developments since Aug 1969. Had these proposals been accepted in full, they would have provided in part at least for recent developments. However the proposed allocation for expenditure, announced on 12 Feb 70 by An Rúnaí has reduced the original Military Proposals by 60% and is considered unrealistic in present circumstances.

Because of the changed Military situation subsequent to 13 Aug 1969, a paper "Requirements of Defence Forces" was submitted on 23 Oct 1969. With some adjustments in priorities this document represents the up to date Military requirements. It sets out the immediate requirements at some £4,500,000 on completion of which a further expenditure of £20,000,000 would be necessary to complete the operational requirements. It is apparent that a reappraisal of the allocations proposed by An Rúnaí on 12 Feb 70 is needed in view of the Government's direction.

Armament

There is a critical deficiency of modern armour, artillery, anti-aircraft weapons and aircraft without which the offensive capability of the forces is negligible. In the present situation the provision of armoured vehicles is a vital requirement.

The present stock of armoured cars is 8 modern vehicles with 8 in Cyprus plus an assortment of 22 old models of very limited operational value. We have no Armoured Personnel Carriers which are of the utmost importance in any operation and especially in the type of operations envisaged.

Combat Vehicles

There is a critical deficiency of small vehicles such as guntowers and Landrovers which are required for mobile radios, reconnaissance and the transport of support weapons. Investigations of the stocks of vehicles of this type in the country show that it would not be possible to make up deficiencies by impressment or hiring.

Signal Equipment

There is a critical shortage of long range and medium range radio sets which are essential to the control of mobile operations.

Ammunition

The position in regard to ammunition is such that if the Defence Forces as a whole were engaged in full scale military operations, the stocks of all types of ammunition could not be expected to last more than a couple of days.

Other Equipment

Considerable deficiencies exist in the case of almost all other categories of military equipment which are essential to military operations.

Conclusions

Implementation of the directive given by the Government on 6 Feb 1970 necessitates the earliest possible procurement of the resources required both in manpower and equipment.

There is obviously a need for reconciliation as between the directive and the sum proposed in the 1970/71 Estimates.

In view of the extreme urgency of the matter I would welcome an early discussion with you.

SECRET"

[NA SCS 650.]

[Attached to this letter is a *Partial Mob [Mobilisation] Plan Code Name: First Step*, also dated 27th February 1970 and referenced SCS 19/1 (reproduced on page 86).

SECRET

GSM 19/1

Br an Chinn Fóirne,

GCL.

27/2/70.

PARTIAL MOB PLAN

CODE NAME: FIRST STEP

Corps	Units	Basis of Allotment	FDF Actual Str				50% First Line				FCA				TOTAL				
			Offrs	NCOs	Men	TOTAL	Offrs	NCOs	Men	TOTAL	Offrs	NCOs	Men	TOTAL	Offrs	NCOs	Men	TOTAL	
INF	Seven Bns	-	115	430	818	1363	103	40	314	457	6	664	2410	3080	224	1134	3542	4900	
ARTY	Seven Bty 7 Tps	1 per bn	43	141	219	403	10	8	48	66	38	187	776	1001	91	336	1043	1470	
CAV	Three Car Sqns	1 per Comd	28	82	183	293	12	5	37	54	-	60	415	475	30	147	456	633	FCA avai 450
CAV	1 Armd Fd Sqn		7	17	16	40	3	1	8	12	-	-	-	-	9	17	71	97	Deficie 2 Offrs 55 ORs
ENGRs	Three Coys	1 per Comd	21	55	142	218	9	6	36	51	6	41	440	487	36	102	618	756	FCA avail 482
S & T	Three Fd Coys	1 per Comd	20	55	90	165	15	3	44	62	-	113	451	559	30	171	585	786	FCA avail 406
SIGS	Four Fd Coys	1 per Comd 1 AHQ	19	68	131	218	6	8	40	54	11	148	365	524	36	224	536	796	FCA avail 321
Fd AMBS	Three Fd Coys	1 per Comd	3	8	3	14	-	-	-	-	45	169	354	568	48	177	357	582	FCA avail 353
MP	Three Grn Coys Six Fd Coys	1 per Comd 1 per Bde	6	231	-	237	5	21	-	26	- 24	- 219	- 244	- 487	18 30	316 462	7 -	341 492	
			262	1087	1602	2951	165	92	527	782	130	1601	5453	7179	352	3086	7215	10653	
Other Units to Peace Estb Str											137	231	907	1335	821	1671	2183	4675	
TOTAL			262	1087	1602	2951	163	92	527	782	267	1892	6360	8514	1173	4757	9398	15328	

The Army's Partial Mobilisation Plan of February 1970

The Government held further secret meetings to discuss Northern Ireland matters on five dates in March: the 3rd, 6th, 10th, 13th and 20th.

The 6th March meeting coincides with a released *Secret* document, which records an encounter between "HR" and Ivan Cooper, the MP for mid-Derry, in which the latter remarked:

> "...he was fearful of serious trouble... this year and was worried about the growing strength of the Ulster Volunteer Force... Catholic policemen could not trust their superiors who often tampered with their mail... minority fears of violence, especially in rural areas, during this year, were well founded... British troops might be able to contain situations in Belfast and Derry but he did not think they could possibly control the rural areas..." (2001/6/513).

On 20th March 1970 "J.G." [James Gibbons] addressed a memo to Secretary Ó Cearnaigh, saying that he would discuss Mac Eoin's memorandum and its documents "with the military and civil sides jointly, before consulting the Council of Defence about it". Secretary Ó Cearnaigh in turn addresses a request to the Army for "the required list as far as the military side is concerned" on 23rd March 1970.]

Comments: Chief of Staff Mac Eoin's memorandum concentrates on one aspect of the two-pronged instruction conveyed by Minister Gibbons on 6th February: the order to prepare to assist the minority by making incursions. It makes no reference to the order to prepare to supply arms.

This detailed *Military Preparedness* document was produced within three weeks of the Directive, which demonstrates that the Army moved with alacrity. The *Conclusions*, too, speak of the *"earliest possible procurement"* and *"the extreme urgency of the matter"*.

One of General Mac Eoin's complaints is that the Army is over one-third below 'establishment', meaning that, though the Government set an aspirational size for recruitment, it consistently prevented the Army from attaining this size by means of financial stringency.

Army thinking is still to plan for large-scale operations, as allowed for in the extensive 'shopping list' we encountered in Chapter 1. In the section, *Effects of Low Strength*, there is reference to *"combat units"*, whilst in that on *Armament*, requirements to enable *"offensive capability"* are outlined; and it is suggested that there is only enough ammunition for a couple days' fighting in the section on *Ammunition*. The Northern incursions are treated as forming something of an invasion, or it is felt that they might lead to more extensive fighting. This planning is more consistent with area defence than rescue missions.

From Document 26 below we learn that Finance Minister Haughey was meeting the General Staff at around this time along with the Minister for Defence. Presumably he was reconciling Government military objectives and Army shopping lists with financial realities.

I cannot say what relationship the Planning Board established in February 1970 has with the one which the Chief of Staff put in place in August-September 1969, which we encountered with three of its Reports in Chapter 1. Certainly we have seen how recommendations of the 1969 Board have already been put into effect and informed the thinking of the Army command.

Document 20: Minister for Defence Stresses Urgency, 23 March

[An unsigned, typed statement, dated 23rd March 1970 appears in the files. It appears to be a minute by Secretary Ó Cearnaigh recording instructions from James Gibbons to himself (Ó Cearnaigh) and General Mac Eoin, expediting implementation of the Ministerial Directive of 6th February:]

"COPY/

23.3.70

An tAire informed C.S. [Chief of Staff] and self that it is feared that there will be a breakdown of law and order in the Six Counties and that willy nilly we will be drawn into it. It is impossible to form any clear picture of what to expect, but the Government visualise the possibility that the lives of Catholics/nationalists may be endangered in some towns & cities. In the case of places near the Border the Government might feel impelled to intervene to rescue those at risk. All this is highly speculative and intervention could only be contemplated as a desperate measure in a desperate situation.

What would be required in men and equipment for such rescue efforts? The Minister would like to go back to the Taoiseach and the Minister for Finance and say we got this instruction from the Government and this is the absolute minimum of equipment that we need to implement it. He would also like to be able to tell them what we can do with the P.D.F. [Permanent Defence Force] and what we can't do in the matter of implementing the instruction. The Chief of Staff considered that very little could be done short of a force of some 15,000 all ranks, which would require mobilisation of 1st Line Reserve and selected F.C.A. This mobilisation would take about 48 hours. While individual training would be of a fair standard, unit training would be virtually nil and would need some weeks of intensive effort after mobilisation."

[NA S 650.]

Comments: Gibbons' essential questions to Mac Eoin here are: *what is the most we can do in the North, given our resources?* and *what additional resources would enable us to do more?*

Though the Minister speaks of *" rescue missions"* in the first paragraph of this minute, he goes on to say: *"He would also like to be able to tell them what we can do with the P.D.F."*, which seems to imply something more than rescue missions.

With these minutes we have further confirmation of a consistent military policy being pursued systematically and with some determination. The fully official nature of the undertaking is again made explicit: Minister Gibbons says *"we got this instruction from Government"*. But at the same time it is clear that there is some delegation within Government. The Minister says he *"would like to go back to the Taoiseach and the Minister for Finance"*. And the Taoiseach being mentioned provides a second confirmation that ***Lynch not only knew exactly what was going on, but was part of the select group carrying out Government policy.***

(Subsequently Jim Gibbons behaved as though he had a hold on Lynch. And he undoubtedly had one after Lynch failed to prosecute him along with other Ministers, which at first seemed likely. But the Taoiseach needed him as a major prosecution witness, one who was privy to the arms importation. We do not know what transpired between the two men but Gibbons was promoted in the Cabinet re-shuffle after Lynch's *coup*. Whatever they agreed, in the event, Gibbons failed to lie systematically enough at the Arms Trial to vindicate the Lynch sackings, and his equivocation made an impression on the jury.)

Again this file note makes no mention of the second leg of the Directive of 6th February: the order to prepare to arm nationalists. There is good reason for this. The Minister would have known that Captain Kelly had that side of things well in hand, and that therefore there was little likelihood of the Army weapons which had been set aside being needed. On 23rd March, while Gibbons was spurring on Secretary Ó Cearnaigh and the Army Chief of Staff, the Department of Finance was ensuring that Customs Officials would not examine a certain cargo from the Continent which was imminently expected at Dublin Port.

Document 21: Ballymurphy Crisis, 2 April

[The Government Directive of 6th February had two aspects to it: preparing for incursions and arming the Northern minority for self-defence. But the two tasks were not necessarily connected. It was not the case that arms were only to be distributed to nationalists in the case of humanitarian intervention by Army units. This is shown by events during the Ballymurphy Crisis of early April 1970, when steps were taken to arm nationalists, but no arrangements were made to deploy troops. Here is General Mac Eoin's account of what happened:]

" g. On 2 April 1990 Minister rang Chief of Staff from NAAS. He indicated that he had received information from Mr Blaney that attacks on the minority were planned and that British Security forces would be withdrawn and accordingly would not afford protection for the minority. The Minister felt that material stored in Dublin should be moved forward

h. On the night of 2 Apr 1970, the following items were stored in DUNDALK military barracks. 500 Rifles, 80,000 rounds ammunition and 3000 Respirators

i. Military intelligence subsequently ascertained that the information given to the Minister regarding reported attacks on the Minority and the withdrawal of British Security Forces were without foundation

j. On 4 Apr 350 rifles were returned to stores in Dublin because of storage problems in Dundalk.
k. Meanwhile the Chief of Staff had formed a small selected planning Board to prepare contingency plans to implement the Government's directive.
...Following intelligence reports, of the possibility of a raid by a subversive organisation on Dundalk military barracks, the balance of 150 rifles and 80,000 rounds of ammunition stored in Dundalk were returned to stores in Dublin on Fri 1 May 1970. "

[NA S650, see Document 24 below from which this account is extracted, and where it forms points *g.* to *k.*]

[This terse report by the Chief of Staff of Army preparations to arm Northern nationalists on 2nd April 1970 was drawn up in early June 1970 for the benefit of Taoiseach Lynch. It does not mention the role of Captain Kelly in the events above. By that time James Kelly was out of the Army and had already been criminalised. Thus Mac Eoin does not mention that Captain Kelly was on the Continent buying weapons which the Government had authorised to be obtained for possible distribution to the Northern minority. Nor that, when it appeared that the Army surplus weapons might have to be handed out after all, Kelly's superior, the Director of Intelligence, attempted to recall him. But the order was countermanded by Minister for Agriculture Neil Blaney—the Cabinet Minister with the closest contacts with Northerners—when it appeared that the arms were no longer needed. The conclusion to be drawn from this incident is that there was a Government plan to arm nationalists for self-defence and that Captain Kelly was its lynch-pin.

Mac Eoin's report would not have been available to Captain Kelly when he wrote his account of the Arms Crisis, which runs over the same incident: the Captain was on an arms mission to the Continent on 1st April 1970. He had been released from routine duties for this purpose. As he was travelling about, his wife, Sheila, provided a contact point. (She was very much in his confidence on these matters, a fact that rankled with Colonel Delaney, Colonel Hefferon's successor as Army Director of Intelligence.) On 2nd of April, when Captain Kelly rang home—

"...She told me that Colonel Hefferon had issued instructions that I should come home immediately because of the situation in the North—it was feared that serious rioting in Ballymurphy in Belfast might escalate. She further informed me that weapons were being sent to Dundalk for possible distribution in Northern Ireland and that I would have to supervise their distribution. I asked her if Mr Gibbons was still in his office. She told me that she did not know, but she knew that Neil Blaney was at home. Accordingly, I booked a call to Blaney's house.

When I got through to Mr Blaney, he told me that the situation in Belfast had improved. I, therefore, suggested that it was not necessary for me to rush back to Dublin immediately and, after some discussion, agreed with Mr Blaney that I would complete my mission on the Continent. I requested him to inform Colonel

Hefferon of this decision" (*Thimble Riggers* p36).

Incidentally, James Kelly goes on to say that on the 3rd April he learned that the first shooting of British soldiers of the Troubles had occurred in Belfast. He comments: "To me, the news of the deaths in conjunction with the Ballymurphy incident made it more imperative that the arms deal be brought to conclusion as quickly as possible" (*Thimble Riggers* p36). The Ballymurphy riots resulted from some heavy-handed Army policing. A lot of tear-gas was used. The Provisional Army Council issued a statement in May 1970, disclaiming involvement in the Ballymurphy riots (*Irish Times* 14.5.70).

[The Ballymurphy Incident was also to feature in the Arms Trial. In the extract below Minister Gibbons is being questioned by Seamus Sorohan, counsel for John Kelly:]

"Mr. Sorohan: Was there a plan to move arms to the Border at the time of the Ballymurphy riots, five hundred rifles to be sent to Dundalk barracks . . . late night moves or decisions in high places or a decision by the Army to send 500 rifles to Dundalk barracks to be in readiness for sending across the Border if needed?

Mr. Gibbons: Do I have to answer this?

Mr. Justice O'Keeffe: It is a proper question.

Mr. Gibbons: I was on my way home to Kilkenny through Naas. I was stopped by the police and asked to ring Neil Blaney who said he had information of the direst kind and had been in touch with Mr. Haughey and at that time somebody was being sent to find the Taoiseach in order to acquaint him of the position and I was requested by Neil Blaney to send certain arms to Dundalk.

I rang the Chief of Staff and, speaking in Irish, said in words to this effect that I had had this request from Mr. Blaney and it might be better to comply with it and ensure that the strictest security was observed at all stages. I think I recall saying that 'If I don't do this, he may do something rash himself'.

Mr. Sorohan: The arms were moved to Dundalk?

Mr. Gibbons: At all times within the Army's keeping.

Mr. Gibbons said that on the night in question the Taoiseach was in Cork. His understanding was that the Taoiseach had goner to his house in West Cork and it was impossible to contact him otherwise than by putting someone in a car to go and see him and he understood, Mr. Gibbons said, that this was being done.

Mr. Justice O'Keeffe: Mr. Sorohan I think you may have gone too far.

Mr. McKenna [chief prosecutor]: All right then, I must ask that the jury be retired in that the last ten questions or so by Mr. Sorohan must have so gravely exceeded the bounds of relevance that there is a grave risk that the jury may, through no fault of their own, be distracted from their primary duty of trying this case..." [*Irish Times*, 25.9.06, p11, c3-4; the omission in the first paragraph appears as in the published report.]

Colonel Hefferon was also questioned about this incident by Captain Kelly's counsel:

"Mr. Finlay: Did you say that the purpose for which you might require him [Captain Kelly] was to assist in the distribution of those arms (the 500 rifles)

because he knew the people in Northern Ireland?
Colonel Hefferon: That is right..." [Ibid, 30.9.1969, p8, c1.]

[Colonel Delaney's rebutting comments, probably drawn up for the prosecution, will be found in Document 30.]

Comments: The Ballymurphy Incident was an important building block in Captain Kelly's defence (and consequently on the defence of the other defendants). The Minister for Defence had to admit that there was a plan to arm Nationalists for self-defence—or at least that the Government had nearly done so on 2nd April 1970. This helped with the 'credibility factor'. Because of Lynch's public pronouncements and his mild profile, it was difficult for many in Ireland believe that his Government had an active military policy which involved giving weapons to civilians in another jurisdiction—which was the core of Captain Kelly's case. But, once it was shown that the Government had sent rifles to Dundalk, with a view to distributing them to Nationalists, that made the rest of the defence credible. Things fell into place. Colonel Hefferon was able to confirm that Captain Kelly was to be the conduit for passing out the weapons. And the need for untraceable arms then became apparent.

It is notable that the Judge immediately intervenes when Mr. Lynch's role in events is probed—and that the State Prosecuting Counsel, Seamus McKenna, here takes his cue from the Judge. The Court went out of its way to prevent scrutiny of the Taoiseach's involvement throughout both Trials.

Document 22: Enemy Strength, 6 April

[Within days of meeting the Defence Minister on 2nd April 1970, the Chief of Staff submitted three copies of a 20-paragraph analysis to the Minister, with Secret typed and stamped on them. The two extra copies were for Lynch and Haughey. A handwritten note added to the covering letter states:

> "Memo. Some time after the submission of this Memo, An tAire (Mr. Gibbons) told me that he intended to give a copy each to the Taoiseach and Min. for Finance (Mr. Haughey)".

Here we have a ***third confirmation of Lynch's close involvement in military preparations*** (NA SCS 650).]

" SECRET SCS 18/1
Oifig an Chinn Fóirne.

6 Apr 70
Copy No. FOUR

Memorandum

Military Commitments and Requirements

OBJECT

1. The object of this paper is to assess the capabilities of the Defence Forces to undertake present commitments, to undertake incursions into Northern Ireland should the Government so determine and to set out the essential minimum requirements in personnel, arms, ammunition and equipment to enable them to carry out these tasks.

2. Scope of paper
This paper is written against the background that the Government may decide to commit the Defence Forces in Northern Ireland should the situation there deteriorate to the point where the lives and property of the minority would be in grave danger.

3. Assumption
It is assumed that the purpose of operations by the Defence Forces in Northern Ireland would be solely towards the protection of the lives and property of the minority, nevertheless, it must be accepted that incursions would be opposed by force.

FORCES AVAILABLE TO NORTHERN IRELAND

4. British Military Forces	Strength
Eight infantry battalions)	5,000 Combat troops
Two Armoured Car Sqns)	1,000 Support troops
One battalion Territorial Army Volunteer) Reserve and Support Troops)	3,000
Ulster Defence Regiment (Ceiling 5,000)	4,000
5. Police	
Royal Ulster Constabulary (unarmed but trained in their use and arms available).	3,500
Ulster Special Constabulary over and above those inducted in the Ulster Defence Regiment	5,000
	21,000

British military forces are fully organised, well trained and well equipped. They have a minimum of 74 armoured cars and 40 armoured personnel carriers. There is a considerable partisan element and arms are available for a majority of a hostile population.

6. Military Reinforcements
Reinforcements available in Britain which could be readily committed in Northern Ireland amount to three infantry brigades, fourteen battalions, three armoured regiments, ten artillery units, two marine commandoes, air support and naval units. The combat strength of ground units which could be so committed amounts to 20,000.

DEFENCE FORCES

7. The following paragraphs set out the strength and assess the present military effectivity of the Defence Forces.

8. Strength

The strength of the Forces in permanent service is 8,860. This figure however includes the Air Corps; the Naval Service; troops overseas, service elements such as the Observer Corps, Medical Corps, Ordnance Corps, Supply and Transport Corps, and Cadets, Apprentices, Band Boys and Recruits in training. Excluding these elements there would NOT be more than 2,500 line troops available to be mustered, organised into units and trained preparatory to undertaking incursions. Particulars of strengths are set out in Annex 'A' attached [not reproduced here].

9. Age

Over 1,700 serving personnel are over the age of 40 years and a high proportion of these would be unfit for front line combat duties.

10. Medical Standard

A total of 560 personnel are in Medical Category C and are unfit for Combat duty.

11. Training

Because of the low strengths of units of the Permanent Defence Force, their dispersal over a large number of permanent posts and border posts and their high incidence of duty, it has not been possible to relieve personnel for essential sub-unit and unit training to fit them for combat conditions. Thus while their individual skills may be described as reasonably satisfactory, they have not received adequate training as part of the team at section, platoon company and battalion levels. Therefore their standard of combat effectivity in present circumstances is low. The standard of FCA training is very much lower.

12. Organisation

Infantry units which would have to provide the bulk of the combat element are generally at one third of their establishment strength. The net effect of this is that it is necessary to reinforce such units or to provide scratch groups made up of personnel from many units in order to provide a minimum acceptable strength for current operations.

13. Warlike equipment

Deficiencies exist in almost every type of armament, ammunition and military equipment. In the context of a possible commitment in Northern Ireland the most serious deficiencies are in modern machine guns, small arms, ammunition, anti-tank ammunition, grenades, gun-towers, landrovers, bullet-proof vests, respirators, combat clothing, radio and other signal equipment. The lack of armoured personnel carriers and the deficiency in modern armoured cars (of which only 8 are available in the country) is particularly serious. The lack of air cover, air support and anti-aircraft weapons could result in our troops being completely immobilised. The details of equipment which would be essential to make good the most critical deficiencies are set out in Annex 'B' [not reproduced here] and would involve a capital outlay of approximately £5 million.

14. Deployment
The detailed deployment of the Forces in permanent service is set out in Annex 'C' [not reproduced here].

a. It will be seen that the full strength available is fully committed on present tasks. Indeed it is already overstretched and depends on the voluntary participation of 677 FCA personnel each week-end on security duties to provide some relief.

b. The protection being afforded at present is confined to 30 installations on which military guards are provided and a further 16 which are covered by motorised patrols. The protection being afforded is minimal and cannot be improved without an unacceptable increase in the already very high incidence of duty being performed, which is currently running in some cases to one 24 hour out of bed duty every three days. Furthermore there are up to 100 other installations which are vital to the community but which are not being provided with armed protection because of the inadequacy of manpower.

ANALYSIS

15. The assessment provided in previous paragraphs of this paper indicates that the armed opposition likely to be encountered by incursions into Northern Ireland is vastly superior in strength, organisation, combat training and equipment to those elements of the Defence Forces which could be mustered for such operations. The superiority in equipment is most critical in armoured cars, armoured personnel carriers and offensive air support which could immobilise our forces. The critical disparity in the combat effectivity of the forces is heightened by the overwhelming capacity of the British to reinforce their troops in Northern Ireland with armour and personnel and their ability to sustain a supply of warlike material which the Defence Forces lack.

16. Incursions into Northern Ireland are likely to lead to counter action such as retaliatory raids across the border against towns, vital installations and military installations and possible reprisals against the minority in areas which could not be reached by our own forces. It will thus be necessary not alone to meet present commitments but to increase garrisons in the border area and to provide additional protection to vital installations. A minimum force of some 15,000 fully trained personnel, organised in units as set out in Annex 'D' attached [not reproduced here] would be essential to undertake incursions at the strength considered necessary, in view of the considerable forces available in Northern Ireland and the necessity to meet other commitments.

17. In view of the present low strength of the Permanent Defence Force it would be necessary to call out the First Line Reserve and FCA on Permanent Service in sufficient time to enable them to be fully trained and incorporated into regular units as set out in Annex 'D'. The provision of such a force can only be regarded as a first step towards a full mobilisation which would be necessary if operations were to escalate. The cost of maintaining such a strength in permanent service would involve additional outlay to the extent of some £6.5 million.

CONCLUSIONS

18. The execution of a directive to mount incursions into Northern Ireland would undoubtedly have the most serious military implications even in circumstances when adequate strength and equipment could be made available.

19. To mount incursions into Northern Ireland on the basis of the existing strength in permanent service would involve stripping all the existing units of active line personnel; mustering them into properly organised formations and relieving them of all duties for intensive training. This would entail the closing of border posts; the withdrawal of military guards from vital installations and the withdrawal of regular support for the training and administration of the FCA. The General Staff could not recommend such a step particularly in view of the fact that the strength of the Force which could be so committed would be inadequate for the task and the depth of its incursions would be extremely limited. Furthermore the withdrawal of personnel from security duties in present circumstances would be a grave risk.

20. The members of the General Staff feel that the Government should be made aware of the disasterous consequences which would follow if such operations were mounted on the basis of present strength and status of supply. Accordingly the members of the General staff request that immediate steps be taken to provide as a first step the personnel necessary to bring the strength in permanent service up to a minimum of 15,000 and the provision of the minimal essential equipment as set out in Annex 'B'.

SECRET"

[Copies are listed as going to the Minister of Defence, the Secretary at the Dept. of Defence, the Chief of Staff, A. Adn., A Crn; CFC and Col. Mattimoe (who must be Cyril M. Mattimoe, Cadet Master, Cadet School in the 1960s). NA SCS 650; no Annexes are reproduced here.]

Comments: Here we have direct confirmation that the Army took any order *"to commit the Defence Forces"* (para *2.*) as amounting to war. The list of deficiencies in *"Warlike equipment"* includes *"anti-tank ammunition"* (para *13.*). A whole section is devoted to examining the respective military capacities of the British and Irish sides: 21,000 soldiers and police versus 2,500 Irish forces, with a further 20,000 British re-inforcements ready, and arms available *"for a majority of a hostile population"* (point *5.*). Given these figures, it is surprising that the Irish command thought another thousand or two on the Irish side could make any difference!

Chief of Staff Mac Eoin is painting the blackest picture possible here: not all the British forces would have been able for combat. But it should be remembered that he is taking a purely military view of the balance of forces: necessarily he leaves politics out of account. While the British Government would not have been happy at an Irish intervention in Northern Ireland to protect Nationalists under attack, such a step, taken in desperation, would have alerted a sympathetic world to the unacceptable political and social arrangements which Britain had put in place in Northern Ireland. It would have changed the situation irrevocably. And, while the intervention would have led to casualties, so did inaction—which in a sense 'privatised' the response to an intolerable situation for the Northern minority, leaving change to be brought about by the necessarily crude methods of the Provisional IRA.

It is clear that *"incursions"* to protect *"the lives and property of the minority"* are envisaged as more than brief rescue missions: that they are viewed as being closer to area defence.

Point *3.* by implication confirms once more that intervention would not be to bring about constitutional change.

Confirmation of delegation within the Cabinet is provided once more by the fact that on 6th April—around three weeks before Lynch's *coup*—Lt. General Mac Eoin submitted a copy each of this Memorandum for Jack Lynch and Charles Haughey, as well one as for the Minister for Defence. This provides a ***fourth confirmation that the Taoiseach had a hands-on approach to military policy***, and that he and his Minister for Finance worked on significant elements of Government military policy either together or with each other's knowledge. (The three previous indications that Taoiseach Lynch was fully involved in framing Government military policy are in: Document 16, the *Addendum*, where Gibbons told the Chief of Staff that the Taoiseach and Government had agreed to the request of delegations for weapons; Document 20, in which Defence Minister Gibbons asked for concrete assessments of Army needs that he could take back to the Taoiseach and Finance Minister Haughey; and Document 22, in which an extra copy of the *Military Requirements* memorandum was submitted for the Taoiseach. (See also reproductions overleaf, which show that the Taoiseach was keeping abreast of confidential reports about Northern Ireland.)

Document 23: Ministerial Procrastination Slated, about April

[The Office of the Minister for Defence produced a *Memorandum For The Government, Review Of The Defence Forces And Defence Requirements* and another document in early 1970, neither of which are reproduced here. These were commented on in April 1970 by Chief of Staff Mac Eoin, who submitted a Secret Memorandum to the Secretary at the Department of Defence in triplicate: thus providing copies for Gibbons, Lynch and Haughey. (It is not being reproduced in full here.)

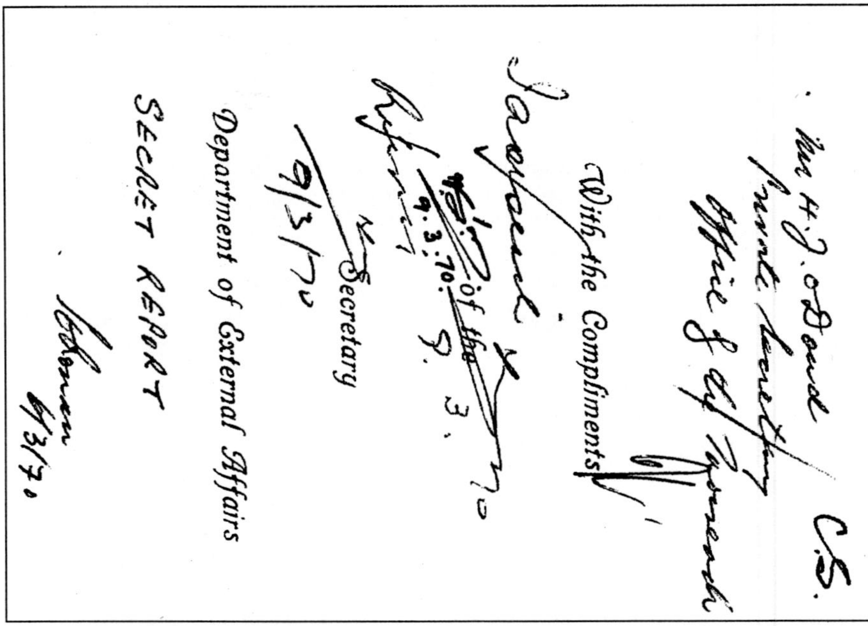

C.S.

Mr H.J. O Donal
Private Secretary
Office of Taoiseach

With the Compliments of the Secretary
Department of External Affairs

SECRET REPORT

9/3/70

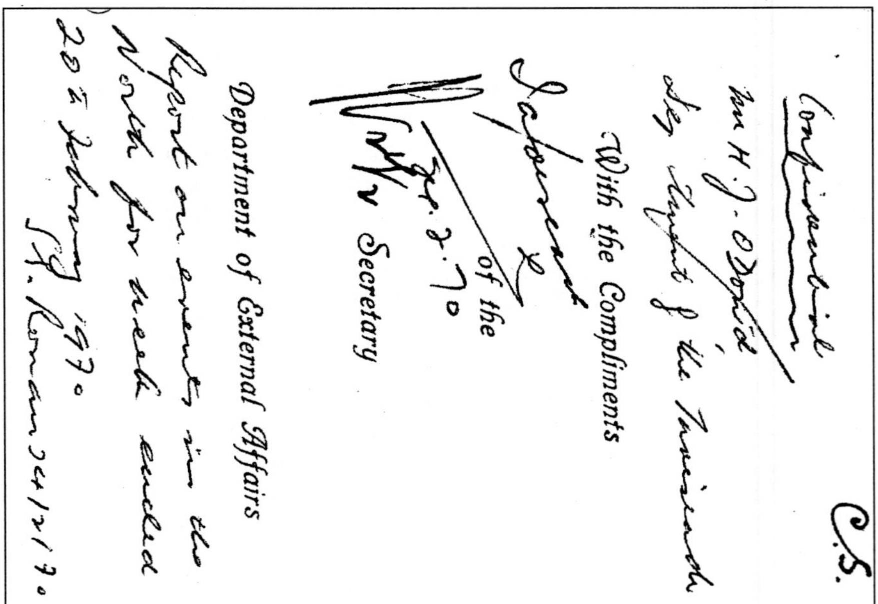

C.S.

Confidential

Mr H.J. O Donal
Sec. Taoiseach

With the Compliments of the Secretary
Department of External Affairs

Report on events in the North for week ended 20th February 1970.

Jack Lynch Keeping Track Of Developments, February/April 1970

Mac Eoin found lacking any "reference to situation last August" Nor did it set out any "mission for the Forces". The document does not meet the "need for a National Defence Policy...", nor for "a procurement policy".

The Chief of Staff pointed out that, despite the title of the Memorandum being "...Defence Requirements", there was a gaping omission:]

> "both papers are incomplete if they do NOT refer to "events in Six Counties" in the past, in the present and in the future. These "events" have high-lighted, and proved beyond all discussion, deficiencies in the Defence Forces in manpower and in equipment. A number of papers have been submitted by the military side, since Aug '69, drawing attention to the position. If "decisions are not being sought at this stage on ammunition, arms and equipment" then one is prompted to wonder what "events" would have to happen so that these decisions might be sought."

[His final paragraph is a complete dismissal of the Minister's document:]

> "Finally, and at the risk of labouring the point, the omission from the Memorandum of any reference to either the "events in the Six Counties" or to any of the military papers submitted since Aug '69 or to the implications of the Minister's directive to the Chief of Staff in Feb 1970, renders the document so defective that, it would be of little value to the Govt. in decisions which they could easily be called on to make."

[NA SCS 18/1.]

[A further secret Cabinet meeting concerned with *Northern Ireland Policy*, for which there is a blank Pink Slips, occurred on 7th April.

Before going on to reproduce further documents, it is worth catching up with events in the political sphere.]

2. Change Of Policy

Towards the end of April trouble appeared, apparently out of a cloudless sky.

First of all, one obstacle after another obstructed the importation of the weapons which had been bought and paid for. The shipment was blocked by sea in March, and then by air in April.

Colonel Hefferon retired as Director of Intelligence, having hung on to the last moment, hoping to see through the Arms Importation. His successor, Colonel Delaney (who we met in the last Chapter as Commandant of the Army's Command & Staff School) had been understudying him since February. He took over practical command on 11th April. For whatever reason, Hefferon did not brief Delaney about Captain Kelly's special mission. He left it to Minister Gibbons to do that. According to Delaney's own hostile account, put together for the Arms Trials, he did not want to retain Captain Kelly under his command.

Meanwhile, Peter Berry, the Permanent Secretary at the Department of Justice, started to interfere. He was long-established, hard-working, very capable, and tended to dominate his Ministers (except Charles Haughey, when he had the Justice portfolio). He was intent on pursuing traditional law and order policies curbing republicanism, and his approach cut across the policies towards the North being pursued by the Government.

Up to that point he had largely confined himself to ordering surveillance, and making reports to his Minister. Now he began to act independently. Vincent Browne published Berry's account of these events in *Magill* posthumously in 1980. Though the report is in Diary form, we are not talking of Diaries written contemporaneously, but of accounts written after his retirement, using his own notes and written in hindsight.

Berry claimed to have been called in by the Taoiseach on 13th April 1970, to give him "a run-down on the IRA situation vis-a-vis the North". He states that when he gave Lynch "the police information about the participation of Ministers in supplying arms to the IRA he seemed to be genuinely surprised" (*Magill* June 1980, p60). Berry was puzzled that his Ministerial briefings had apparently not been passed on. (As for his claiming that the weapons were for the IRA that is a result of seeing what was going on with Treatyite blinkers: the Irish Government's military policy was to arm minority areas.)

On 17th April, Berry learned of the attempt to import arms by plane and set up plans to arrest those involved and capture the arms. At this point he took over executive authority from the Minister, and did not even keep him in touch with what he was doing.

After a cryptic telephone conversation with Haughey on 18th April, Berry decided that it revealed that "Government qua Government were not behind the arms conspiracy". He telephoned the President (who has no administrative role in Government) and got his authority to bypass his Minister and go to Lynch directly about the plot he thought he had discovered and did so on 20th April.

A secret Cabinet meeting concerned with *Northern Ireland Policy* occurred on 21st April. It is marked by a blank Pink Slip.

Charles Haughey had a very serious riding accident on the morning of 22nd April 1970, which left him with severe concussion and broken bones.

On the same evening Micheál Ó Moráin created an incident at a Dublin legal function and admitted himself to Hospital for treatment. (Government military policy had put him in a difficult position *vis a vis* Peter Berry and it is possible that he was drinking heavily as a result.)

Berry had further encounters with Lynch. What went on between the Taoiseach and the chief civil servant at the Department of Justice, behind the back of the Minister of Justice, is a subject of dispute. Berry subsequently wrote an account of it which became public, but Lynch neither confirmed nor denied it, being overcome by amnesia. However he did not deny that, at this critical moment in the affairs of the State, he discussed the affairs of the Ministry of Justice with Berry behind the back of the Minister. By doing so he made himself effectively his own Justice Minister.

In these circumstances, in late April, with two senior Ministers incapacitated, Lynch enacted an unannounced change of policy. He forced Ó Morain to resign on health grounds. And he dismissed his Ministers for Finance and Agriculture (Haughey and Blaney) on the grounds that they disagreed with Government policy—a thing which journalists close to the Government had got no hint of until then. A short time later he had them charged with criminal conspiracy against the State.

Kevin Boland, Minister for Local Government, resigned from the Cabinet in disgust at Lynch's action, as did a Junior Minister, Paudge Brennan.

On 28th April Captain Kelly was suddenly transferred out of Intelligence by Delaney and Gibbons. He was told by the new Director of Intelligence to desist from his Northern activities, while Gibbons urged him to continue them. He felt he was being subjected to constructive dismissal. Suspecting perfidy—that he might be held incommunicado in a military prison—he submitted his resignation from the Army *"voluntarily"* on the next day. His resignation became effective on the 1st May and he was immediately arrested by Special Branch and held overnight for questioning. Refusing to make a statement he was brought to see first Minister Gibbons and then Taoiseach Lynch. After a night in a filthy jail cell he was released without charge, but expecting further trouble.

A secret Cabinet meeting on *Northern Ireland Policy* was held on the day that Captain Kelly was transferred out of Intelligence.

Jack Lynch forced Minister for Justice Michaél Ó Móráin to resign on grounds of ill-health on 4th May. The new Minister for Justice was Desmond O'Malley.

There was a secret Cabinet meeting dealing with *Northern Ireland Policy* on 5th May, as indicated by a blank Pink Slip.

William Cosgrave, the Leader of the Opposition, approached the premier with an anonymous message, apparently emanating from the Garda, on 5th May. Charles Haughey and Neil Blaney were dismissed on 6th May. They were subsequently arrested and charged.

James Gibbons was promoted from the Department of Defence to the Department of Agriculture. His last day as Defence Minister was 9th May. The new Minister was Gerry Cronin, promoted from Parliamentary Secretary at Agriculture.

The change in Government policy had happened by means of a *coup* by the Taoiseach.

A secret Cabinet meeting considered *Northern Ireland Policy* on 12th May, again marked by a blank Pink Slip

(We will examine the detail of these matters in the next work in this series, on the Arms Conspiracy Trials.)

3. Army Responses

There can be little doubt that Lynch's abrupt alteration of Government policy came as a bombshell in the Army. But very little has come into the public domain about that. All we have is straws in the wind: rumours of Army moves. But in general the Army received Lynch's moves quietly, and took his statements on trust. However, it is a fact that Taoiseach Lynch was very worried about how his sackings of three Cabinet Ministers closely associated with Northern policy (and the resignation in sympathy of a fourth, Kevin Boland) would be received by the Army. Colonel Delaney, in a file note, records receiving a phone call from the Minister for Defence in the early hours of the morning of Thursday 7th May, asking about Army attitudes to the arrest of Captain Kelly.

Having purged his Cabinet and debated the reasons for doing so in the Dail, did Jack Lynch call in the Chief of Staff and indicate that the Army may have been misled about Government military intentions by Cabinet Ministers delegated to handle Northern Ireland affairs?

The evidence shows otherwise.

And, indeed, it is hard to see how he could have disclaimed what had gone on. As we have seen, communications to the Army implicated the Taoiseach in the erstwhile active military policy towards the North.

Clearly Lynch had a job to do to make sure that the Army command did not give him grief at a time when prosecutions were pending on matters consequential to Government decisions.

Jack Lynch therefore arranged to meet the Chief of Staff on 9th June 1970. And General Mac Eoin prepared for the meeting by preparing an appropriate summary of Army activities as regards the North. And he ended his report with a very substantial section analysing military pay—which had been overtaken by inflation and which the Army had been campaigning to have raised for a long time.

4. More Documents, 1970

Document 24: Mac Eoin Prepares To Meet Lynch, 5 June

[A comprehensive brief was put together for the Chief of Staff, so that he could make the most of this rare meeting with the Taoiseach. Presumably he made a submission to the Taoiseach based on its contents. It recorded what the Army has been doing on Government instructions since mid-August 1969. But Mac Eoin took this golden opportunity to lecture the premier about Government failure to provide the Army with the resources needed to do its bidding:]

"   TOP SECRET   SCS 18/1

BR CEANN FÓIRNE,
CCA.
5 JUN 1970.

BRIEF FOR CEANN FÓIRNE

1. DEFENCE POLICY

a. The lack of a clear-cut Governmental Directive on the form, which Defence Policy should take has created a considerable degree of uncertainty and frustration within the Defence Forces. No long-term procurement policy in regard to personnel or equipment can be drawn up in such a climate.

b. Critical deficiencies in personnel strength, and in equipment allied to the present very high incidence of duties have created a situation in which training for combat is not possible. In these circumstances combat efficiency is very low.

c. Following a directive from the then Taoiseach in June 1962, various major studies were initiated by the General Staff. These were

Ireland in a Major War	1962
Defence Policy Memorandum	1963
Defence Review Board Report	1965
Defence Policy Memorandum	1967

These documents were very comprehensive; they examined every facet of the Defence Forces, suggested roles and responsibilities and set out the requirements of the Defence Forces to implement these.

d. None of the papers above have been submitted to the Government.

e. The events since August 1969, have only served to confirm the lack of combat effectivity. When no one unit could from its own resources provide an effective force and when it became necessary to form ad-hoc groups hastily drawn together and made up from personnel from administrative, technical and training staffs to provide sufficient numbers to protect and support the refugee centres and field hospitals [sic].

f. Early examination of the military submissions by the Government is essential and urgent coupled with a clear-cut directive, as to the mission of the Defence Forces, the designation of their roles and responsibilities and a clear statement as to the means in manpower and equipment which will be made available to them.

g. A brief appraisal of the capabilities of the Defence Forces is referred to in Paragraph 2 of this paper and is set out in Appendix I attached [not included here]. "

[Thus far, the Brief is typed. It now switches to handwriting (by Lt. Col. J. Adams), and the pages are stamped Secret:]

"2. Situation in Northern Ireland

a. In August 1969 following on civil strife in Northern Ireland, the Defence Forces deployed three hastily formed infantry groups along the border to support and protect Field Hospitals and Refugee Centres.

b. Following a directive from the Minister for Defence, the General Staff had an "Estimate of the Situation" prepared which assessed the situation in Northern Ireland and the capabilities of the Defence forces to provide more positive assistance should the strife in Northern Ireland continue at the level of mid August 1969 or even deteriorate. The assessment indicated a very low standard of combat effectivity, and a critical situation in regard to personnel deficiencies and shortage of essential equipment, which precluded action.

c. In November '69 the Defence Forces took over from the Gardai the commitment of protecting certain vital installations threatened by Ulster Volunteer Force activity. The Defence Forces still retain this responsibility in addition to their other commitments. This has forced a reduction in the strength of units deployed near the border . In spite of these reductions the incidence of duties, particularly 24 hour-out-of-bed duty, is very high and places a considerable strain on morale.

d. At 1630 hours on Friday 6 Feb 1970 the Minister for Defence informed the Chief of Staff and the then Director of Intelligence that the Government at a Cabinet Meeting on that date had instructed the Minister to order the Chief of Staff to prepare and train the Army for incursions into Northern Ireland if and when such a course became necessary, and to have respirators and arms and ammunition made ready in the event that it would be necessary for the minority to protect themselves. The Minister explained that the Taoiseach and other Ministers had met delegations from the North. At these meetings urgent demands were made for respirators, weapons and ammunition, the provision of which the Government agreed as and when necessary. Accordingly the Chief of Staff was instructed to put truck loads of these items at readiness so that they could be available in a matter of hours if required. The Minister asked the Chief of Staff the nature of the most critical deficiencies of the Defence Forces, to which the Chief of Staff replied

Manpower
Armoured fighting vehicles
Transport

The Minister instructed the Chief of Staff to hold himself in readiness to discuss estimates with Mr Haughey on his release from hospital.

e. A military study of the directive was undertaken and the Chief of Staff sought a meeting with the Minister on 13 Feb 1970 to seek clarification as follows..."

[The questions and answers listed appeared above as Document 17. The document continues:]

" f. On 18 Feb 1970, the following items were assembled in Dublin and Athlone..." [These appear above as Document 18.]

" g. On 2 April 1990 Minister rang Chief of Staff from NAAS... [There follows the account of shifting weapons to Dundalk during the Ballymurphy Crisis, which appears above as Document Twenty-One.]

SECRET"

[NA S650]

[The 'Brief' switches back to typing for Section 3, entitled *Revision Of Pay, Pensions, Gratuities And Allowances.* This two-page "Confidential" section reports the complete failure of a Ministerial Working Party established on 24th April 1969 on the Army request for a Pay Commission, with the consequent resignation on 25th May 1970 of "A Crn". An Appendix shows Comparative Rates Of Pay at various ranks with the Garda and Civil Service.]

Comments: There is a duality evident in this Brief over Government orders to the Army over preceding months. While sticking to the cover story over the August 1969 deployment, "to protect and support the refugee centres and field hospitals", the Brief goes on to clearly outline the Government Directive of February 6th, and the actions taken by the military in consequence.

The document also mentions an *Estimate of the Situation*, prepared by the Army following a *"directive"* from Minister Gibbons (at *2.b.*), which I have not seen. The date of this is not mentioned, but it can be taken to have been prepared between August and November 1969—the dates of the preceding and succeeding paragraphs, that is, in September-October 1969. It assessed *"the capabilities of Defence forces to provide more positive assistance should the strife in Northern Ireland continue at the level of mid-August 1969 or even deteriorate".*

It is also specifically pointed out that the 6th February Directive ordered that arms were to be made ready for the eventuality *"that it would be necessary for the minority to protect themselves"* (*2.d.*), and gives a detailed account of the measures that were taken. That cannot be something that Lynch would have wanted to be reminded of at that particular moment.

As backing for the Army's case for more resources, the *Brief* mentions that the August 1969 deployment to the Border was only possible after assembling mongrel units, composed of soldiers fit for combat drawn from a variety of other deployments (*2.e.*).

The general assumption in this *Brief* is that the orders to the Army remain in being and that military policy has not changed.

So, what attitude did Jack Lynch take during the conference to which he has called the Chief of Staff? Was he about to tell him that the 'incursion' policy, along with schemes of arming nationalists, died with the Cabinet expulsions—or even that these mad schemes were the result of a subversive plot concocted by an Intelligence Captain in alliance with errant Cabinet Ministers—the line for public consumption?

Document 25: Mac Eoin / Lynch Encounter - One, 9 June

[The conference of 9th June 1970 was attended by Taoiseach Lynch, new Minister of Defence Gerald Cronin, Lt. General Mac Eoin, and the Permanent Secretary at the Department of Defence (*Runai Roinn Cosanta*).

It is hard to imagine the state of mind of the Army Chief, going in to this meeting. The Government had lost four leading members of Cabinet, two of whom were charged on 27th May with Conspiracy to Import Arms. Others charged include one of Mac Eoin's most capable officers, Captain Kelly, as well as a leading member of the Citizens' Defence Committees, John Kelly, and a civilian, Albert Luykx.

There are two Minutes available. The Department of Defence account is a mostly typed summary, while the Army minutes comprise a hand-written document marked "Secret". Here is the brief Departmental account, which is part of a more general report, only the relevant part of which is in the file:]

> " *Meeting with Taoiseach on 9-6-70*
>
> 3. The Taoiseach gave a clear exposition of the Government's attitude regarding military requirements in relation to the Border situation viz., that the sending of troops to the Border last August was to provide hospital facilities for persons needing treatment consequent on the disturbances in the North and to provide protection for the Army Field Hospitals. This had already been made clear in his various public statements. The Taoiseach also recalled the Government's attempts to have a joint Irish/British presence in the North. However, it was necessary to consider what should be done in case there was a major breakdown of law and order in the Six Counties and plans should be laid for this eventuality. It amounted to a question of doing all we could, with whatever resources we could muster, to rescue Nationalists whose lives were in great danger. The Chief of Staff gave an account of military studies of this problem and the requirements for rescue incursions into the Six Counties on a limited scale. He mentioned a figure of about £5,000,000 for equipment and a strength of 15,000 personnel. The Taoiseach said he would mention it to the Minister for Finance."

[NA]

Comments: The reason Jack Lynch is explaining why the Government sent the Army to the Border in August 1969—10 months previously—is that he is indicating that he is sticking to the cover story—as though history could be re-wound and re-played differently!

As for the reference to *"a joint Irish/British presence in the North"*—that concerns a second cover story in August 1969: this time to 'explain' the calling up of the First Reserve. (We saw Patrick Hillery use it to Lord Chalfont in Pamphlet One of this series.) But those extra troops remained called up even after it became clear that there would be no deployment in association with Britain or with the United Nations.

While Lynch does not disavow the Government Directive of 6th February, he emasculates it into *"rescue incursions into the Six Counties on a limited scale"*. But, as we saw in Document 17 (reporting questions from the Chief of Staff to Minister for Defence of 13th February), the original Government plan was far more ambitious. At point *(2)* the following exchange took place:

"The Military assume that the sole object of incursions would be the protection of the lives and property of the minority	The Minister confirmed that such was envisaged"

We also saw the formulation of protecting *"lives and property"* used in Document 22 (para 2), which assessed the balance of military force.

Intervening to protect lives and property implies that personnel could be involved in area defence. There is a world of difference between 'rescuing' people and defending them.

Similarly, the second leg of the Directive of 6th February, to be prepared to arm the minority, has got lost. That point, too, was specifically addressed during the meeting of 13th February:

"(12) With regard to the arms, ammunition and respirators (a) How many are to be made available (b) To whom and in what circumstances are they to be handed over	The Minister had no idea but agreed that stockpiles were to be held in Dublin and Athlone"

Despite the emasculation, the general order to the Army to be ready to intervene to assist nationalists still appears to stand. What Lynch feared above all at this point is that there might be a repeat of the serious disorder of the previous Summer, when lives were lost and there was widespread ethnic cleansing, with a whole street burnt down. His *coup* could not have survived such an eventuality. Hence his orders to the Army that it should be ready to prevent any repetition.

That was the Government account of the meeting between the Taoiseach and the Chief of Staff. Let us now look at how the other side saw the meeting.

Document 26: Mac Eoin / Lynch Encounter - Two, 9 June

[The hand-written Army minutes for the same meeting of 9th June 1970 provide a far fuller account:]

" <u>SECRET</u>

Meeting With An Taoiseach   Rn P & O

C.C.A.

Tues 9 Jun 1970 16 Jun 70.

Present

An Taoiseach
Aire Cosanta
Ceann Foirne
Runai Roinn Cosanta

1. An Taoiseach indicated his pleasure at the meeting with An Ceann Foirne and expressed his regret that pressing business had prevented his having a meeting sooner.

Defence Policy

2. An Ceann Foirne referred to the lack of clearcut Governmental policy on defence and indicated the urgency of this matter apart altogether from the situation in the North of Ireland. At this stage however he was not prepared to go into detail. He felt that he should fully brief the new Minister as a first step on the question of defence policy generally.

3. In the various studies made of the defence situation, An Ceann Foirne emphasised that Northern Ireland was examined in the following contexts
a. as an area which could provide the Western Bloc with a secure land base from which hostile operations could be mounted against the State
b. as an area from which assistance could be expected in the event of an Eastern Bloc invasion of the State.

4. In view of the reiteration of Government policy from time to time regarding the aim of reunification of the national territory by peaceful means, no military studies had been undertaken nor had plans been prepared even on a contingency basis for military action in Northern Ireland prior to August 1969.

Northern Ireland

5. The Taoiseach recounted the events of last August in which the following military deployment took place, and enquired if the Chief of Staff was satisfied with and clear on the tasks set. The Chief of Staff replied that he was
a. Field Hospitals were set up in Rockhill, Fort Dunree, Dundalk, Castleblaney and Cavan.
b. Refugee centres were set up in Gormanstown, Finner Camp and Kildare
c. Casualty collection points were set-up forward of the field hospitals and mobile patrols operated between the casualty collection posts and the field hospitals and refugee centres.
d. About 1000 troops were deployed in Dundalk, Gormanstown, Castleblaney, Cavan, Mullingar, Longford, Finner Camp, Rockhill and Fort Dunree to protect and support the field hospitals, the refugee centres and the casualty collection posts.

6. The Taoiseach enquired if the field hospitals were open still. An Ceann Foirne replied that the equipment and beds were in location but that the personnel had been withdrawn. They could however be reactivated at very short notice.

7. In further reply to the Taoiseach, An Ceann Foirne indicated that an overall reduction in the strength of troops in border posts had been effected and he outlined the present approximate strength in each.

8. Direction of 6 Feb 1970
a. In reference to the direction of 6 Feb 70, which was made known to An Cearn Foirne by the Minister for Defence (Mr James Gibbons) and which required the Army to be trained and prepared to make incursions into Northern Ireland, the Chief of Staff had assumed that these incursions would be made in circumstances in which there would be a complete break-down in law and order in which the lives of the minority would be in grave danger and in which the Security Forces in Northern Ireland would be unable or unwilling to protect the minority.
b. The Taoiseach confirmed that the circumstances envisaged by the Government were those assumed by the Chief of Staff.
c. Regarding the use of the term "incursion" the Chief of Staff explained that this term had been used in conveying the Government directive and that it conveyed to him that cross border activity was not intended as an invasion but rather as a short temporary stay to carry out a mercy mission and return.
d. Further to the discussion at c above the Chief of Staff indicated that a military study had been compiled involving an incursion to Newry. This Northern town, which although considered to be close to the border is considered as the extreme limit of incursion capability at present strength and status of supply. The study indicated that some 800 troops would be necessary for such an operation; that the stay might well have to be limited to 24 hours at most and that even then considerable casualties could be anticipated.

9. The Taoiseach re affirmed that it was the policy of the Government that force would NOT be used as a means to re integrate the national territory. He recounted the various means used by the Minister for External Affairs to bring the matter before the United Nations Organisation. While Dr. Hillery had advocated the presence of a United Nations Peace Keeping Force which would include Irish troops, the Government had not been very hopeful that such a course would be acceptable to the British Government.

10. The Taoiseach himself had given considerable thought to the possibility that Irish troops could work in conjunction with British troops in the event that a situation would arise in the future in which the British troops would be unable to defend the minority. In reply to a question by the Chief of Staff the Taoiseach indicated that should incursions into the North be required, they would not be preceded by political or diplomatic representations.

11. Capabilities of Defence Forces
a. The Chief of Staff referred to the very limited capabilities of the Defence Forces in view of critical deficiencies in manpower and equipment and he informed the Taoiseach of the military proposals to incorporate the F.C.A. into a "First Step" organisation which would provide some 15,000 personnel, which in the military view was the minimum force necessary if incursions were to be undertaken.
b. The Taoiseach was aware of meetings which took place between the

General Staff and Mr Gibbons and Mr Haughey. He was also aware that further meetings had been planned. He was more familiar with the situation in regard to the deficiencies in equipment than he was with the state of deficiencies in personnel. He was of course aware that the standard of Combat training was low. He stated that he would arrange to have the new Minister for Finance meet the Minister for Defence and the Chief of Staff on the question of personnel and equipment at an early date.

SECRET"

[NA MI 5 p2-8.]

[The minutes originate in the Planning and Operations Section, Army Headquarters (*Rn P & O, CCA*). A *Routing Slip*, dated 23rd and 25th June 1970, indicates that MacEoin has approved these minutes of his meeting with the Taoiseach. It is addressed to Col. S.C. Ó Donnabháin/Donovan, Director of Planning & Operations (*S/P&O*), and signed by Lt. Col. J. Adams. The note adds that the Chief of Staff directs that he "be kept reminded to raise the question of arms and ammunition with the Minister" (Ibid).]

Comments: Like the Government minutes, Mac Eoin's account features the 'light' version of the deployment to the Border of mid-August 1969 and of the Directive of 6th February 1970.

In Point *5.* we are reminded that the Government has altered the traditional policy of disregarding the North.

The Army minutes shed light on how the Army understood the orders to prepare for incursions. Mac Eoin explained that forces could not be sent further into the North than Newry (a largely Catholic town, which is about 10 minutes' drive from the Border), and that, even for such a limited exercise, 800 troops would be needed. Even a force of this size might not be able to maintain itself for more than 24 hours (point *8.d.*). This estimate sounds conservative, to say the least! It suggests that nationalists could expect very little help from the Irish professional military in protecting their lives if they chose not to flee trouble.

This assessment shows why the Irish Government thought—until outside forces dislodged it from this view—that it was important to provide nationalists with the capacity to defend their own areas.

The idea of *"protecting"* the *property* of the minority has disappeared altogether as any explicit task, and the suggestion that forces would probably not be able to stay more than 24 hours bears that out.

At *8.c.* Mac Eoin defined *"incursion"* as *"a short temporary stay to carry out a mercy mission and return"*. It is hard to imagine what use such a capability would be, beyond escorting people out of danger areas. The 'Siege of Derry', for instance, lasted for some days. Again, as in two documents cited above (Document

17 *(2)* and Document 22, para *3.*), the implication is that reassurance is being sought that constitutional change is not the objective of military intervention.

Lynch responded to the implicit question by saying that the Government has ruled out force to unite the national territory (point *9.*). That is true, and was a view held unanimously (including by Ministers Haughey and Blaney). There is a world of difference between providing area defence in places like Derry and Newry during a crisis and invading the North with a view to conquering it.

With paragraph 10 we are back to Lynch's dream scenario: that a Protestant backlash to reforms would force Britain to ask Ireland to help police the North. But Britain took great care never to push things too far, too fast. Naturally the minority was frustrated at the slow pace of change, and by what often appeared as favouritism towards the majority community. But, as we shall see in later in this series, ruling circles held the view that Catholics had to be given a hammering in the particular, so that civil rights reform might proceed in the general.

As in the meeting with Minister Gibbons (Document 17) Chief of Staff Mac Eoin asked the Taoiseach whether diplomatic representations would be made before any Army incursion. Was he presenting his own view that there should be in the form of a question? However, Lynch's approach remained the same as Gibbon's, despite all that happened: if there were incursions, that represented a failure of existing approaches to diplomacy.

More generally, MacEoin knows and Jack Lynch knows that those being criminalised (Captain Kelly, John Kelly, Albert Luykx, Charles Haughey and Neil Blaney) have been implementing policy authorised by the Cabinet. The Chief of Staff is not able to counter what is being done by the Taoiseach without causing fundamental damage to the State itself—which he is sworn to uphold. But perhaps Mac Eoin was wondering whether the Army could reap some material benefit, in terms of much-needed upgrading, from the circumstances in which the Taoiseach currently found himself?

Jack Lynch obviously had to exercise tact in handling the military men in the new situation, after prosecutions had been set in hand with Lynch's change of tack. The meeting with the Chief of Staff was undoubtedly a signal mark of favour: Army/Taoiseach meetings were rare. The intention was to draw a line between the orders to prepare to prepare for incursions, and those to prepare to distribute arms to nationalists along with Captain Kelly's arms purchasing activity.

There was another carrot coming. The Cabinet agreed on 14th July 1970 to implement pay increases recommended by a Working Party. And the pay rise was to be back-dated over a year, to 1st June 1969 (NA 2000/6/659).

Documents Twenty-Seven: Incursions: Planning Continues

[Even in July 1970 the planning assumption was that there might be incursions into Northern Ireland. By 1st July 1970 no further funds had been made available to the military to enable preparations for Northern interventions to proceed, despite the Taoiseach's assurance, so Secretary Ó Cearnaigh addressed a memorandum to his Minister about the matter:]

Document Twenty-Seven (a)

"*S E C R E T*

Aire.

Referring to the discussion with the Taoiseach on 9th June about the Defence Forces' position in relation to the Six-County situation, you will recall that the Taoiseach visualised the possibility of an extreme situation arising in which the Government might feel impelled to employ the Defence Forces on rescue missions across the Border. The concept of a peace-keeping force of Irish and British troops was also adverted to. The Taoiseach wished to know what preparations would be necessary to meet these contingencies. The Chief of Staff mentioned a requirement of equipment amount to £5,000,000 and 15,000 personnel.

The Taoiseach's resumé of Government thinking confirmed statements made by your predecessor in March last, as a result of which the Chief of Staff submitted to Mr. Gibbons three copies of a Memorandum dated 6th April 1970 on "Military Commitments and Requirements". Mr. Gibbons told me at the time that he intended to give a copy each to the Taoiseach and the Minister for Finance, but apparently he did not get round to doing so.

At the meeting on 9th June the Taoiseach said that he would ask the Minister for Finance to consider the financial implications. I am not aware of any further developments.

It is not quite clear where the initiative now rests but in order to clarify the position I suggest that you write to the Taoiseach on the lines of the attached draft."

[NA S650.]

[A tactful way has been found of prodding the Taoiseach and the Minister for Finance into action about the promised funds to enable military preparations to proceed: re-giving them Mac Eoin's report produced on foot of the February/ March directives of the Government to prepare for incursions.

The new Defence Minister, Jerry Cronin, thereupon writes to Mr. Lynch on 1st July:]

Document Twenty-Seven (b)

"S E C R E T

1 Iúil 1970
Dear Taoiseach

Referring to the discussion in your office on 9th June at which the Secretary, Department of Defence, and the Chief of Staff were present, I find that my predecessor had taken up the question of the possible involvement of the Defence Forces in rescue missions in the Six Counties should a very grave deterioration in the situation there occur. As a result the Chief of Staff prepared a memorandum dated 6th April 1970 entitled "Military Commitments and Requirements", of which copies Nos. Two and Three are attached.

I understood at the meeting on 9th June that you would speak to George Colley about the financial implications. Meanwhile, until I know whether the contingency plans are financially feasible, I am afraid there is no action I can usefully take."

[The letter was addressed to Seán Ó Loinsigh Uas TD (Jack Lynch). NA S650.]

Comment: In the Government minutes of the Lynch/Mac Eoin meeting Lynch used the term *"rescue"* to describe Northern missions. Mac Eoin spoke of *"rescue incursions"* (Document 26). Minister Cronin above finds a new term, *"rescue missions"*, in this letter! However, while there is a world of difference between an *incursion* and a *rescue mission*, the general order remains in being.

Document 28: Financial Curbs, July

[I have found no record of this appeal bringing any immediate results. George Colley (Haughey's successor at the Department of Finance) produced a proposal to keep spending in each Department the same, but adding an amount for pay increases, inflation and a slice of any increased funds that might be available. The Department of Defence took exception to this procedure in a paper called, *Notes on the Memorandum for the Government dated 16 Iúil, 1970, submitted by the Minister for Finance on "Forward Planning of Government Finances - Allocations for 1971-72"*. Essentially the Finance proposals are slated for being woolly and not allowing the Defence Forces the extra resources required to meet Government demands and upgrade.

The submission to the new Finance Minister, dated 23rd June, protests about his proposed "method of allocation" of funds. Under Colley's scheme "The Department might never receive enough to make an impact on the "capital deficiencies" (NA SG50).

A covering "Secret" memo dated 23rd July from P.M. Ó Cléirig, Assistant

Secretary at the Department of Defence, to Minister Cronin, passes on these remarks from the Department of Defence, stating—

> "In addition to the matters mentioned in the Notes, which refer to the need to repair the serious deficiencies in the equipment, transport etc. of the Defence Forces in normal circumstances, you will, no doubt, advert to the special needs referred to in An Rúnaí's secret minute to you dated 1 Iúil, 1970, a copy of which is attached for your convenience" (NA S 650).

An Rúnaí's minute of 1st July is Document 27 (a).

Document 29: Funding Needed, 30 July

[Inability to meet the demands on the defence forces, given present resources, is raised yet again with the Minister of Defence by Chief of Staff MacEoin on 30th July. This points out that retirements from the First Reserve now mean that the Army does not have as many resources available as it did in August 1969:]

" *SECRET* SCS 29

Br. An Chinn Fóirne.

30 Iúil, 1970.

Aire Cosanta.

Critical Deficiencies in the Defence Forces.

Recent events in N.I. indicate that the situation there can no longer be regarded as a temporary flare up, but one that may be expected to continue for some years with growing intensity and serious implications for the country as a whole.

In many submissions over the past few years, and particularly in the past twelve months, the General Staff has drawn the attention of An tAire to the general unpreparedness of the Defence Forces to undertake the scale of operations which the security of the State may dictate. It has been made clear that this state of unreadiness to meet possible commitments stems mainly from critical shortages in manpower and material brought about by financial constraints on Defence expenditure.

The requirements of the Defence Forces to meet the demands of the present situation and to provide for possible future developments have been clearly set out in SCS 29 of 27/2/70 and SCS 18/1 of 6/4/70. I feel it my duty to point out that instead of an improvement being effected, I must report a steady deterioration in our operational capabilities.

Following the call-out of the First Line Reserve last August the total number on permanent service reached the figure of some 9,658 all ranks. The current figure is about 8,778.

The comparative position is as follows:-

	PDF				FIRST LINE RESERVE				TOTAL			
	Offrs	NCOs	Ptes	Total	Offrs	NCOs	Ptes	Total	Offrs	NCOs	Ptes	Total
Aug 69	1073	3043	3930	8046	253	230	1129	1612	1326	3273	5059	9658
June 70	1059	3029	4397	8485	32	37	224	293	1091	3066	4621	8778

At the moment there is some degree of temporary easement by FCA units which are on annual training but this easement will terminate in August i.e. the end of the FCA Summer Training Period. Thus from August the strength in service will be about 900 less than the strength in August 1969. In the interim demands on the Defence Forces have greatly increased.

Since the end of Oct 1969, the Def Forces have been committed to the protection of vital installations which involves

Fixed guards at 29 locations
Mobile patrols to 14 additional installations

This task, alone, stretched the resources of the Defence Forces beyond the limit of estimated capabilities making very heavy demands on an already inadequate supply of men, transport and communications equipment. In June of this year a further demand was made on the Army, when the Government directed intensification of patrolling in the Border area in order to have a degree of surveillance along the entire length of the Border. A Government direction of 6 Fea 70 required the Def Forces to prepare for possible operations. In addition to these commitments the normal training programme for the PDF and FCA must be maintained. Thus compared with August 1969 the Def Forces have more commitments with less manpower and material resources.

I must now emphasise that it is the opinion of the General Staff that unless urgent action is taken to make good the deficiencies in trained men and material, the time will come when the Defence Forces will no longer be capable of meeting even their present commitments.

RECOMMENDATIONS

In order to carry out current and possible future tasks the following action is necessary.

1. Recruitment to be commenced and continued until the PDF is brought up to Peace Establishments. Such a recruiting drive, in order to succeed, must incorporate real incentives such as improvements in conditions of service.
2. As an interim measure pending the induction of recruits to bring the PDF to an acceptable strength, to allow the employment of FCA on security duties in excess of the figure permitted by the existing financial limitation of £84,000.
3. Extraordinary financial provision for the procurement of essential military equipment, particularly transport, communications equipment and armoured vehicles.
4. Implementation of a scheme whereby the management of installations would play a more positive role in their own internal security to complement protective measures..."

[NA SCS.]

Comments: The *"incursions"* to Northern Ireland of the 6th February Directive have now become *"possible operations"*. Nevertheless, the instruction to be prepared for action on the other side of the Border has not been rescinded.

The reference to increased Army surveillance duties on the Border follows an arrangement made by Lynch with the British authorities as a way of defusing a situation resulting from a number of British Army incursions over the Border following incidents with republicans.

Document 30: Colonel Delaney's *Real-Politik*, 5 October

[At the September 1970 Arms Trial Colonel Hefferon caused consternation by testifying as to the contents of the Government Directive of 6th February. He also gave other evidence which exonerated Captain Kelly.

Official files record the strenuous efforts Col. Hefferon's successor as Director of Intelligence, Col. P.J. Delaney, made to assist the prosecution in damage limitation. On 5th October 1970 he prepared a *Memo* in which he commented on the Government *Directive* of 6th February (Documents 15 and 16 above), and on the *Brief* preparing Mac Eoin for his meeting with Lynch (Document 24). In paragraphs *4.* and *5.* below he claims to be speaking on behalf of Chief of Staff Mac Eoin, which leaves the reader to assume that the whole document represents Mac Eoin's views:]

Document 30a

"

TOP SECRET
MEMO
From : Army Intelligence
Date : 5 October 1970

. . .

4.a. With regard to paragraph 2 b and c of the Ministerial Directive [of 6th February, Document 15 above; reference to provision of respirators and arms] the Chief of Staff wishes it to be known that at the time he received this Directive he understood these paragraphs to mean :

> "that these respirators, surplus arms and ammunition were to be used as Government Policy as directed".

b. This is further clarified by paragraph 2 d of "Brief for Ceann Foirne" [Document 24 above] which states inter-alia :

> "At these meetings urgent demands were made for respirators, weapons and ammunition, the provision of which the Government agreed as and when necessary".

c. This also clarifies paragraph 2 d of the Directive [Document 15: this paragraph says the exact nature of the Directive in regard to *2 b.* and *2 c.* was not mentioned; paragraph *b.* said "Respirators ?", while paragraph *c.* said "Weapons and arms, surplus ?"].

5. The Chief of Staff further wishes it to be understood that paragraphs 2 a, b and c of the Directive of 6 February 1970 [which ordered preparation for Army incursions and to arm the minority] and the items mentioned at paragraph 1 b of Addendum to Memo of 10 February 1970 [arms demanded by Northern delegations] were to be used only in the context of and having the meaning shown at paragraphs 2 e (i) and (ii) of "Brief for Ceann Foirne" which clarification had been given by the Minister for Defence on 13 February 1970.*

[* Paragraph e is reproduced above as Document 17, in which points (1) and (2) are as follows:

" (1) The Military assume that incursions would only be mounted in circumstances where there would be a complete break-down of law and Order in N. Ireland and where the Security Forces were unable or unwilling to protect the Minority	The Minister confirmed that such a situation was what was envisaged
(2) The Military assume that the sole object of incursions would be the protection of the lives and property of the minority"]	The Minister confirmed that such was envisaged

6. a. In view of the SECRECY requirement in paragraph 2 e (5) of "Brief for Ceann Foirne" how could Colonel HEFFERON instruct Mrs KELLY to instruct Captain KELLY who should not know of this plan to return from the Continent to distribute the 500 rifles sent to Dundalk on 2 April 1970. As well paragraph 2 e (5) states :

"The Minister indicated that the Northern delegations had not been informed of the Directive to the Defence Forces". [Document 17 above. Paragraph 2 e (3) excludes diplomatic representation before action.]

b. Had Colonel HEFFERON and Captain KELLY and others a secret plan for this operation unknown to the General Staff ?

c. How can Colonel HEFFERON's action in instructing Captain KELLY to return from the Continent to distribute the 500 rifles be reconciled with the following :

"At about 1800 hours on 2 April 1970 the Chief of Staff came into the Lounge in McKee Barracks where there was a going-away party for Colonel HEFFERON and told Colonel HEFFERON and Colonel DELANEY that the Minister had telephoned from NAAS etc. etc. On hearing this Colonel DELANEY suggested that certain Staff and Commanders should be sent for at once. This was done. Soon after this the Chief of Staff asked Colonel DELANEY to whom were these supplies to be given and asked if there was a distribution plan. Colonel DELANEY replied that he knew absolutely nothing of the operation but suggested to the Chief of Staff that he would ask Colonel HEFFERON who was standing a little distance away. Colonel DELANEY put the same question to Colonel HEFFERON who said he knew absolutely nothing either. Colonel DELANEY communicated Colonel

Hefferon's reply to the Chief of Staff.

7. Paragraph 6 of this MEMO should be reconciled with paragraph 2 e (12) [Document 17] where the Minister indicated that he did not know who the surplus arms, ammunition and respirators were for. The actual situation and state of affairs in the North at the time of the BALLYMURPHY riots were not as Mr. BLANEY gave them to Mr. GIBBONS at NAAS on the evening of 2 April 1970. See paragraph 2 g and i of "Brief for Ceann Foirne". [2 g,2 h and 2 i describe the weapons movements in connection with the Ballymurphy incident, see Document 21.]

8. Colonel HEFFERON did not hand over Captain KELLY's activities to Colonel DELANEY.
...

9. Captain KELLY performed his "duties" directly to Colonel HEFFERON making sure that no one in the office got any wind of what was happening.
..."

[NA MI 2]

Comments: Two different matters are bundled together in this document. The first points reproduced above represent (allegedly) the views of the Chief of Staff. The rest is composed of Colonel Delaney's own ideas. But the one passes seamlessly into the other, giving the impression that these points represent the views of Mac Eoin as well.

A different picture of Mac Eoin's view of the Court proceedings is conveyed by the following story, told by Harry Boland (the brother of the Cabinet Minister who resigned in protest at Lynch's Cabinet dismissals):

> "After one particular disgraceful episode by the then Minister for Defence [Gibbons], my brother, Kevin, who had been Minister for Defence when first elected to Dail Eireann, was leaving the Court, which he had attended each day, the former Commander in Chief, General McEoin, turned to him and said "wasn't that nauseating"..." (*Irish Political Review*, September 2006).

In fact the Chief of Staff attended part of the Arms proceedings, but then left for Cyprus to inspect the Irish UN contingent. Whether this was to avoid being called as a witness, or in disgust at the behaviour of the Government, I do not know.

Point *6.a.* attempts to put Col. Hefferon in the wrong: he either breached secrecy by informing Mrs. Kelly of a State secret which even Captain Kelly was supposed not to know about or he was perjuring himself when he said he instructed the Captain via his wife to return from the Continent to distribute Army weapons during the Ballymurphy Crisis.

At point *6.b.* the Director of Intelligence asks whether Hefferon and Kelly had a *"secret plan"*, unknown to the General Staff, thereby implying that they had and that it was unauthorised.

The fact is that there was a *"secret plan"*, but it was the Government's plan. At present there is no way if knowing who in the Army was privy to it. Certainly, only a minimal number of Cabinet Ministers knew of it in detail. But General Delaney's idea in mentioning a *"secret plan"* is to promote the idea of an illicit plot.

Points 8. and 9. are directed towards confirming the idea of 'funny business' by indicating that Hefferon did not pass on details of Kelly's mission to his successor, and that Kelly himself reported personally to the Director of Intelligence, excluding other members of the Intelligence section from his reports. However, Colonel Hefferon explained in the Court proceedings that the project in hand was so sensitive that he felt it was entirely up to the Minister of Defence to initiate his successor as Director into Government plans. We have only Col. Delaney's word for it that the Minister did not do so.

The Government dealt with Hefferon's 'treachery' in telling the truth (or as much of it as was necessary to exonerate Captain Kelly!) by seeking to discredit him.

A similar kind of point is made in another released *Top Secret* document, which is not reproduced here, *Arms Conspiracy Trial. An Examination of some of the Evidence pertinent to or directly concerned with the Army* by *Army Intelligence* [NA MI 2]. This quoted counsel for the prosecution, Mr. McKenna, asking Col. Hefferon who was Captain Kelly's superior, "entitled to give him orders as to duties". In that document, Col. Delaney writes:

> "Colonel HEFFERON replied: "In this particular case I consider he was acting on a Government Mission".
>
> On further questioning Colonel HEFFERON answered this question by saying the Minister for Defence was Captain Kelly's superior officer. Again, on further questioning, Colonel HEFFERON agreed that between January and April 1970 Captain KELLY was under his - Colonel HEFFERON's - own orders.
>
> 4. Comment
>
> ...it was never officially and authoritatively arranged through the responsible officer, the Adjutant-General of the Army, that any Minister - Finance, Agriculture or Defence - would assume direct control over Captain Kelly and issue him orders, other than his official military superior, Colonel HEFFERON..."

In a further point, No. *26.*, Delaney suggests that if Kelly could be said to be carrying out "Government Policy" on Col. Hefferon's orders, that authority ended after Col. Delaney took command, when Kelly continued the importation mission without reporting to Col. Delaney.

Colonel Delaney is here misconceiving the unique position of the Irish Army at the time, which was under direct political control which could circumvent the normal chain of military command.

While denying that Captain Kelly had any special relationship with Ministers as a result of the Mission he was given in August-September 1969, Col. Delaney explained in the same document that, while he wished to have the officer removed from Intelligence, he was anxious that he be given a good alternative position, to avoid "giving him a grievance and perhaps causing him to compromise the office". This would indicate that he knew very well that Captain Kelly had information of a very special nature, compromising to the Government and the Army.

In the event, Captain Kelly took the change of Government tack and his forced resignation from the Army on 1st May very quietly. Even after the Ministerial sackings and revelations in the Dail, he made no public statement until his own name and reputation were traduced by the authorities.

As for the story about Hefferon's retirement party (Document *30.*, *6.c.*), Col. Delaney is being disingenuous. Not one of the documents reproduced above contains details of who it was planned to give weapons to in the particular—though the question did come up from the Army side a couple of times. What was known in general was that the arms were for the people represented by the numerous delegations that were canvassing Ministers (and not just the Government but the political parties and the Trade Union movement).

As for Hefferon saying he *"he knew absolutely nothing"*, what else could he say, when questioned about a closely-guarded Government secret in an insecure environment? It might be that he did not know all the specific individuals through whom arms would have been channelled. But it would be very surprising if he could not have hazarded a fairly accurate guess, given the fact that Captain Kelly made regular comprehensive reports of his activities—reports which went to Government.

When he wrote this *Memo*, Col. Delaney would have been aware of Col. Hefferon's Trial testimony indicating that he and Captain Kelly had agreed that the arms that were being brought in from the Continent would be stored in a monastery on the Border, pending Government instruction that distribution should proceed. This evidence, which convinced the jury, indicated that both Col. Hefferon and Capt. Kelly men were working under official instruction.

I am puzzled by Col. Delaney's observation in point *7*: that paragraph 6 should be reconciled with the Minister's statement to the Army on 13th February that he did not know who the weapons were for (Document 17). Taken at face value, the essential message of these two statements is that the Minister of

Defence was arranging to send arms North, but did not know who they were to go to. They raise the question as to why Gibbons was not on trial too! Is that what Delaney was hinting at here?

But the fact is that Minister Gibbons knew very well, as did Col. Hefferon, that weapons were intended for the Citizens' Defence Committees in the North. It just did not suit them to say so in the particular circumstances of the retirement party described above.

Document 30b

[In a separate document, Colonel Delaney comments on the *Government Directive* (Document 15), and on the *Addendum* (Document 16):]

" SECRET

MINISTERIAL DIRECTIVE

1. Colonel HEFFERON was at first meeting between Minister and Chief of Staff on 6 February 1970 but was not at Army Staff meeting held on 11 February 1970 .

2. It is most unlikely that Colonel HEFFERON or Captain KELLY or any other unauthorised person has possession of the Ministerial Directive or relating documents as :

   a. all these documents were numbered copies and were in their rightful locations after Colonel HEFFERON left the Army,

   b. Captain Kelly was not given an opportunity of getting them after Colonel HEFFERON retired,

   c. Colonel HEFFERON would not have asked Colonel O'DONOVAN [Director of Planning and Operations] for information out of them if, in fact, he had photostats or manuscripts of them in his possession.

3. The Directive should not be released because of the contents of paragraph 2.a [prepare Army for incursions]. This paragraph standing alone is open to misinterpretation.

4. The suggested planning procedure as outlined at paragraphs 4a, 4b, and 4c was not put into effect as far as present Director of Intelligence [Delaney] is aware. However, a Conference similar to that as outlined at paragraph 4b did take place subsequently.

ADDENDUM

5. It is emphasised that paragraphs 1a, 1b and 1e of Addendum can NOT be released because NO Government can afford to publish openly what could be called its normal SECRET military plans especially if these plans are directed against a friendly State. Such a revelation in open Court would cause a diplomatic furore of the first order. This is just NOT done by any State, regarded as friendly.

6. Paragraph 1c of Addendum is very important as it shows that there was not a deficiency of Pistols. There was a deficiency of :

Manpower)
Armoured Fighting Vehicles) as mentioned by the Chief of Staff
Transport)

...

FILE FOR SUMMARY OF EVENTS 13 AUGUST 1969 TO 1 MAY 1970

8. The relevant paragraphs here are e(1), e (2), e(3) , e(5) and e(12), also paragraphs i, j and m. This document cannot be released because of the significant contents of these paragraphs.

9. However, paragraph e(3) is the most significant. It should never be revealed that incursions were to be made into Northern Ireland in defiance of the UNITED NATIONS Charter, in contravention of international codes of behaviour, and without having at first notified the friendly power and having gone through the normal diplomatic procedure to be expected from a nation with a good and respected role in Peace Keeping throughout the world. Since the operation did not take place, it would be totally wrong and unnecessary to reveal at this point in time that it was the SECRET intention to carry it out without at first having consulted the friendly nation.

TERMS OF REFERENCE FOR PLANNING STAFF

10. This document cannot be released except in part.

11. Paragraph 4 should be released in part i.e. ".....the planning Staff will base its plans on the existing strength of the Forces and the equipment and armament currently available to them." It is vitally important that the above sentence be publicised in some way as it gives the lie to the allegation by Colonel HEFFERON and Captain KELLY that the Directive was a "back-up" for the purchase of Pistols. In fact this sentence gives a direction totally opposed to that notion.
The Chief of Staff could NOT have inserted the above extract in his guide to the Planning Staff unless he got this direction from the Minister. This clearly shows that the Minister and the Government did NOT associate or create the Ministerial Directive as an authority for or as a "back-up" for the purchase of Pistols and ammunition.

SECRET"

[NA MI 5/3]

Comments: A careful reading of this document appears to indicate that Col. Delaney is treating the minutes of the meeting of 6th February 1970 [Document 15] as being the Government Directive. The points he mentions refer to those minutes. I have no way of knowing whether the Government put its orders into writing, as requested by the Army command.

In points 1. and 2. Colonel goes to some trouble to establish that neither Col. Hefferon, Captain Kelly, nor anyone favourable to the defendants, has a copy of the minutes of 6th February. This suggests that he thought the information in them would in fact exonerate the defendants.

Captain Kelly noted on his copy of this document: *"Col Hefferon took notes"* of the Directive; also *"Hefferon briefed me on DIR. at time of issue"*. As to Col. Hefferon's requesting to see the original: *"He wanted exact copy in P & O [Planning & Operations] for trial where he was prosecution witness"*.

Delaney's suggestion that none of the defendants had the exact Directive sheds light on a curious event connected with the Arms Trials, in which the Directive was declared 'lost' by the prosecution when the Defence sought it for the abortive Arms Trial in September, but which was 'found' during the October Trial. Here is what Kevin Boland says about this matter:

> "I have not dealt with the mysterious matter of the 'lost and found' transcript of the verbal directive about possible incursions into the Six Counties, which was given by Mr. Gibbons to the Army on the direct instructions of the Government. I don't intend to go into it in detail as I believe Tom McIntyre's diary of the Arms Trial 'Through the Bridewell Gate' gives the incident its correct perspective and, in the event, it was no more than a side issue. There are just two aspects I think I should mention. It was stated in the abortive trial that the transcript which the Defence wanted to be produced, could not be located. I think few people could have believed such an important document could have been mislaid in Army H.Q. During the second trial Mr. Gibbons himself volunteered the information that it had now turned up. For a time it appeared as if the defence were now being challenged to repeat their request for it to be produced. In fact, it had been rewritten in the meantime in the office of Mr. Gibbons' successor [Mr.Cronin] with the assistance of phone calls to the Taoiseach. Apparently it was felt that this "reproduction" could safely be produced in court, but when the matter was further considered wiser counsels prevailed. The Chief of Staff, to whom the verbal directive had been given, and who had dictated the original transcript and whose evidence would have been necessary to authenticate the document, was Lieut. General Sean McKeown, who had served with distinction as United Nations Commander in the Congo and who was known to be a man of absolute integrity. After the existence of this document had been made known in court I received information and was able to make one of the Defence counsel aware of the rewriting of the document, of the people present when it was done, of the name of the Army Officer, who actually wrote it down, and of the phone calls to the Taoiseach. Whether this became known or not, there were other rumours of other meetings in connection with the rewriting of the document and, obviously, another senior Army officer (or maybe two) of the calibre of Col. Hefferon as witness would be disastrous. The document was not produced; Lieut. General McKeown did not appear on the witness stand; instead he went to visit the troops serving in Cyprus and, when his term of office as Chief of Staff expired, he was not reappointed. He was succeeded by Col. Delaney who had also succeeded Col. Hefferon" (*Indivisible Faith* p236).

Tom McIntyre, in the book which is referred to by Boland, suggests that the Directive was rewritten after the first Trial was abandoned, and that Jack Lynch was involved:

> "...The (prevailing) south-west wind, however, does murmur of a week-end meeting in a coastal resort—not so long ago—involving the witness [James Gibbons], the Attorney-General [General Condon] and the present Minister for Justice [Gerry Cronin), the Directive—that which was lost and hath been found large in their considerations. No commencing prayers, we may assume for Colonel's Hefferon's well-being. What can we do with the Directive? And after much deliberation, continues the south-west wind, there was a journey made to far west Cork, to the removed spot where broods the Taoiseach, far from enemies. Can you hear him greeting the visitors—'Welcome, Gentlemen', about him his usual air of a man who is thinking of going to confession. Into the cottage. The wives—it's a respectable week-end—follow, one of them (much travelled) remarking of the rocky surrounding landscape that it bears a remarkable resemblance to Mexico—were it not for the rain. Women, as the poet says, get under things" (*Through The Bridewell Gate*, 1971, Faber & Faber, p108).

This is rather vague, but seems to be based on the testimony of someone who observed part of the encounter.

*

Col. Delaney hand-wrote the following *Top Secret* file note, which seems to indicate that the Military Directive could have been removed from Army HQ over the weekend of 2nd to 6th October 1970, that is immediately before the second Arms Trial was due to start:

> "Mr Cronin Minister for Defence telephoned Col Delaney during his lunch-break at AHQ on Friday 2 October and told him that Mr Gibbons Minister for Agriculture required Some [sic] papers in connection with a Directive issued around 6th Feb 1970. Mr Cronin gave authority to have those papers given to Mr Gibbons.
>
> Col Delaney informed the Chief-of-Staff of the Minister's Decision. The Chief of Staff told Col Delaney that he was to bring these papers to Mr Gibbons.
>
> Col Delaney telephoned Mr Gibbons & informed him of what the Chief of Staff said. Col Delaney brought the papers to Mr Gibbons on Monday 5 October.
>
> TOP SECRET"

[MI 5/3]

This account seems rather a rigmarole if the proceeding was innocent. This is not a simple business-like note, recording what was being done with sensitive papers. The note has a subjectivist air to it which sounds most unmilitary.

What the memo certainly shows is that the prosecution witnesses were given special privileges. Micheál Ó Morain was not allowed to consult his Departmental papers, prior to the Trial, though a Prosecution witness, nor was another Prosecution witness, Col. Hefferon, allowed to check the wording of the Directive.

*

Whatever about these stories, it is certainly true that the Directive was highly damaging to the prosecution case; that the prosecution could not find it during the first Trial, but suddenly found it was available during the second. But, as Kevin Boland says, if the minutes of the Directive, Mark I or Mark II, had been produced to the Court, General MacEoin would have had to authenticate them and, if he had been put into the Witness Box during the trial, he would be open to cross-examination over Cabinet instructions to the Army.

I would assume that Kevin Boland would not have published his allegations if he was not absolutely convinced of their truth: this was a man honourable in an old-fashioned sense that is rare nowadays.

Colonel Delaney's careful note above about who would have known what in points *1.* and *2.* of the Ministerial Directive carries the sub-text that it would be safe to produce a Bowdlerised form of the Directive.

Delaney, in point *3.* suggests that the Directive should not be released because of paragraph *2.a.*, the Order *"to prepare and train the Army for incursions into Northern Ireland"*. He desired this suppressed because it was open to *"misinterpretation"*. As no political tendency was proposing a war of reconquest of the North, the only *"confusion"* it could generate would be an enlightenment in favour of the Defence case that the Government had authorised the covert supply of arms to the Northern minority.

In Point 4, Delaney seems to be denying that the Directive was taken seriously. But, after denying that the Staff Conferences set out in the Directive minutes took place, he admits that one did.

The documents reproduced above indicate the contrary of what the Director of Intelligence suggests: They show the Army taking the Directive very seriously indeed. Lt. Gen. Mac Eoin told Lynch that a planning board was immediately established, and he quoted one of its findings: that Newry was the furthest reach of any overt operation.

The suggestion that Pistols (which is what the Defendants were charged with importing) were not on the list of Army deficiencies presented by the Chief of Staff to the Minister (Point 6) is nothing more than a debating point. Captain Kelly noted on his copy of this document: *"Why were not [Army pistols] put on one side? They would have been more useful in urban area like Belfast than rifles that were sent to Dundalk. Also they would have been untraceable as was discussed at early stage (See Hef's evidence)"*. Another comment was written in: *"They [the pistols] were purchased by a rep of CDC [Citizens Defence Committees] & became my responsibility in Jan/Feb with authy [authority] of Minister"*.

Colonel Delaney became prey to political correctness in Points 5 & 9, when he suggests that Government plans were in breach of international norms of good behaviour. As an officer who had served on a UN Peace-keeping mission in the Congo, he should have known better about how States behave in the world. The Secretary-General of the United Nations, Dag Hammersjold, died in a very mysterious air-crash because he was obstructing American Cold War politics in the Congo.

Though straying on to the political field with his remark about how States behave, the Director of Intelligence ignored the situation of mayhem that this *"friendly state"* had made inevitable with its arrangements for governing Northern Ireland, and which Irish Government plans were seeking to address. Captain Kelly noted on his copy: *"The mission was to protect Irish citizens, which most Nationalists claimed to be".*

Moreover, if that Government did not want its contingency plans made public, why on earth did it bring prosecutions which made it inevitable that they would come into the open? Did Lynch expect the defendants to allow themselves to be led quietly to the scaffold?

Captain Kelly made comments on this point: *"It was State brought matter to Court. It could have called off operation", "It was government initiated arms trial & opened up matters", "It was Govt mounted charges—brought affair to public notice".*

There is a rather distasteful *realpolitik* evident in Col. Delaney's memos—one which underlay the whole of the prosecution case and the subsequent Public Accounts Committee hearings. Those demonising the defendants knew very well that they were innocent of the charges brought against them. However, they conceived that the interests of the State—with the added consideration, in the case of the Public Accounts Committee hearings, of petty party advantage—required an injustice to be done.

I have not seen two documents mentioned by Colonel Delaney, *File For Summary Of Events 13 August 1969 to 1 May 1970* and *Terms Of Reference For Planning Staff.* His references indicate that they are in keeping with the documents reproduced above and even more damaging to Lynch's position.

Point 11 contains denials of a point which I believe goes to the heart of the Defence case. Originally, there was no intention that the Army, in the shape of Captain Kelly, should become involved in the large-scale supply of weapons to the Northern minority. The Government provided funds through a Relief Fund set up in August 1969, and Intelligence Officers were deployed in an advisory, liaison and coordination capacity. However, those attempting to purchase big quantities of weapons for the Citizens' Defence Committees ran into difficulties with British Intelligence and in negotiating with continental arms dealers. Captain

Kelly was asked to provide assistance in arms purchase. The exact sequence of those events will be examined in a further publication. Here we need only note that Colonel Hefferon felt that such an extension of his remit could create difficulties for the Army and advised his subordinate to consult Ministers about how to proceed. It appears to me that the Directive of 6th February 1970 was the ultimate result of that consultation: the Cabinet instructed the Army to become involved in supplying weapons to the Nationalist minority. Colonel Delaney is aware of this authority and that is why he denies *"the Directive was a "back-up" for the purchase of Pistols"*, and *"the Minister and the Government did NOT associate or create the Ministerial Directive as an authority for or as a "back-up" for the purchase of Pistols and ammunition"*.

And Delaney's only proof for these strong denials is a phrase he quotes from the *Terms of Reference* (which I have not found), which indicates that the armed forces should base their plans for incursions into Northern Ireland on *existing strength and resources*—the implication being that the Arms Importation operation was superfluous! A drowning man clutching at straws!

Captain Kelly noted against Point 11: that the underlined words *"could not"* and *"unless"* were a "doubtful surmise", and also: "Based on assumption Not the definitive statement or conclusion it attempts to imply".

5. *Summary Of Documents*

The fourteen documents reproduced in Chapter One showed how the Army considered the various military options for helping the minority in Northern Ireland and found that, while some overt Army assistance was possible though problematical, covert operations, and arming and training of Catholics for their own defence presented little difficulty. The sixteen documents in this Chapter are overwhelming in their testimony: first of how the Government started down the road of providing overt and covert military assistance to the minority in the North, and then how it pulled back.

Captain Kelly, John Kelly, Albert Luykx, Charles Haughey and Neil Blaney were arrested on 27th May. They were to be charged with conspiring with people unknown to import arms and ammunition in contravention of the *Firearms Act* between 1st March and 24th April 1970. Calling the project a *Conspiracy* made it far more serious in legal terms: simple illegal importation of arms carried minimal penalties.

Now readers have had a chance to consider the thirty documents reproduced so far, they can judge for themselves what the *conspiracy* was and who the culprits were. It is clear to me that any *"conspiracy"* there was started in late April, and it involved bringing false charges against many of those most instrumental in carrying out Government policy up to that point. And the documents show what that Government policy was.

Document 15 reproduces the *Government Directive* to the Army, with instructions *"to prepare and train the Army for incursions into Northern Ireland"*, along with orders to prepare respirators, arms, and ammunition for distribution.

An *Addendum To Government Directive, Document 16*, makes it clear that the Directive was from the Cabinet, and that Taoiseach Lynch was amongst those who had received *"delegations from the North"* and promised them weapons.

Army Questions to the Minister, listed in *Document 17*, established that the Army *incursions* were to protect *"the lives and property of the minority"*. No diplomatic representations were to be made before the Army moved.

The list of Army weapons set aside for the Northern minority, which appears in *Document 18*, is substantial: 500 rifles with 80,000 rounds of .303 ammunition and 200 machine guns with 99,000 rounds of ammunition.

Document 19 sets out Army requirements if incursions are to be mounted. The lack of "modern armour, artillery, anti-aircraft weapons and aircraft" is complained of—without these *"the offensive capability is negligible"* (from Armaments sub-section). It is concluded that: *"Implementation of the directive given by the Government on 6 Feb 1970 necessitates the earliest possible procurement of the resources required both in manpower and equipment"*.

The need to move urgently is stressed by the military in *Document 20*.

Document 21 shows hurried Army shipment of weapons and respirators to Dundalk on 2nd April 1970, in keeping with the Directive, and shows that arming the minority was in no way contingent on Army incursions into Northern Ireland. Captain Kelly's role is highlighted by Col. Hefferon's court testimony indicating that there were moves to recall Capt. Kelly from his Arms trip to the Continent, in order to distribute Army weapons to Citizens' Defence Committees.

The Chief of Staff submitted a further urgent plea for military resources to the Government in early April 1970, *Document 22*, sets out the respective strengths of the Irish and British sides, and pleading for extra personnel and *"Warlike equipment"*.

Ministerial procrastination on upgrading the armed forces is slated by the Chief of Staff in *Document 23*.

Even after the arrests, Cabinet sackings, and criminal charges, the Government Directive still appears to stand. Taoiseach Lynch does not disavow it in his meeting with Lt. Gen. Mac Eoin on 9th June, or blame the military policies of previous months on errant Ministers or Army officers. We have the *Brief For Ceann Fóirne* (Chief of Staff), *Document 24* dated 5th June, which runs over the military developments since the Directive of 6th February, and which continues to mention the instruction to arm the minority.

The minutes of the Mac Eoin/Lynch encounter (*Documents 25 and 26*), however, fail to mention the arming of the minority, and the incursions have been reduced to brief interventions when nationalist lives are in danger: protection of property has disappeared.

Despite this, planning for incursions on these diminished lines continues, with the Army fencing with the Dept. of Finance to get the necessary resources (*Documents 27-29*).

Document 30 provides an insight into the seamy side of the *Conspiracy*, with Colonel Delaney providing debating points, arguments, and spurious facts to the prosecution in the Arms Trials. Despite launching a criminal process, the Government is intent on suppressing the truth about its military policies over preceding months.

6. Conclusion

The picture of Irish Government military intentions in 1969-70 revealed by these documents contradicts the prevailing view of the Arms Conspiracy Trials. It is one that the Army itself has yet to come to terms with. Lt. Colonel John P. Duggan wrote a history of the Irish Army which glosses over the biggest event in Army life since the Second World War in a very misleading way. Though he didn't have the benefit of document releases, he had 37 years' service (1939-1976), with a subsequent academic training. After his retirement he obtained a History Degree at UCD and M. Litt at TD under Dr. Patrick Keatinge (Dept. of Political Science). Here is what Duggan wrote:

> "In 1969 the outbreak of violence in Northern Ireland over-shadowed normal work to a very great extent. It constituted a greater menace to the State than the IRA eruption in the 1950s which had necessitated the reintroduction of internment. New Establishments had to be prepared, new units deployed, vital installations protected…
>
> Initially, UN operations in Cyprus and the Middle East were maintained. A three-phase mobilisation scheme was planned. Planning studies and liaison with Civil Defence continued. Something had to to be done about the inadequate stocks of all types of ammunition and explosives. The chronic low-strength problem came to a head in August 1969 when it became necessary to call up the First Line Reserve.
>
> To further frustrate matters infantry battalion organisations were constantly changing, causing confusion in staff Tables and in accounting for weapons and equipment. Command staffs had to contend with peace, mobilisation, UN Infantry group and home-based Infantry group organisations, most of which were dissimilar…
>
> Another defect in military preparedness was the scarcity of young officers and NCOs. The average age of officers was forty-two and of the NCOs forty and a half.
>
> Internal security situations were not new…
>
> To meet the immediate threat at home in August 1969 the 14th, 15th and 16th Infantry Groups were quickly formed and quietly deployed in Dundalk,

Castleblaney, Cootehill and Cavan. The requirement to provide personnel for these new groups at instant notice, as well as for UN Cyprus contingents and many other activities, in addition to maintaining the training and administration commitments of permanent and FCA units, placed a severe strain on resources. Marshal Foch listed public opinion as a principle of war. It was a resource that now had to be cultivated. Consequently, while for security reasons the Infantry groups deployed silently, more publicity was given to the establishment of refugee camps and field hospitals. The Defence Forces found themselves involved in a newly expanding role, of providing, in changing times, a new dimension of traditional aid to the civil power—a complex operation.

The primary responsibility for the maintenance of law and order rests with the civil power, the Garda Síochána. Provision also exists in law for the Defence Forces to aid the civil power if needs be. Since 1969 subversive threats to the very institutions of the State have proclaimed this need. The IRA have carried out raids for weapons and military equipment, large-scale robberies on banks and cash in transit, kidnappings of prominent businessmen, riots and foundations of public disorder and the illegal importation of arms and equipment" etc. etc." (*A History Of The Irish Army*, 1992, pp279-80).

This is not the place for a detailed analysis of this sketch of military developments after August 1969. Suffice it to say that this account deliberately runs together a thirty-year period in a way which gives an unsuspecting reader to understand that the Irish Army mobilisation of August 1969 'faced inwards'—that it was required to protect the State from an internal IRA campaign. The tone is set by reference to the 1956-62 IRA campaign, and is underlined by reference to *"internal"* problems, *"at home"*, and *"aid to the civil power"*.

One does not need access to *Secret* documents, nor any military background, to know that military mobilisation followed Jack Lynch's promise of 13th August 1969 not to *"stand [idly] by"* while the Northern minority was attacked, and that the military moves were directed outwards, towards the North. This is known to those who lived through the crisis, and can be traced from the newspapers of the time.

The attempt to portray the events of 1969-70 as resulting from any IRA campaign is ridiculous. And it is laughable to suggest that military mobilisation was in response to any kind of *"internal"* threat.

The fact is that the crisis had its heart in the North: republicans did not create it (and the Provisional IRA did not even exist at the time). While all sorts of elements played a role in the movement to emancipate the Catholics of Northern Ireland, the civil rights agitation was bigger than any tendency within it, or even than the sum of all of them. The 'Siege of Derry'—the immediate occasion for Army mobilisation—is not mentioned at all by Lt. Colonel Duggan in his Chapter, *Aid And Assistance (From 1969)*, nor is the Civil Rights context of the crisis.

F.X. Martin OSA supplies a brief Foreword to the book, in which he several times stresses that the Irish Army is "not an aggressive... Force". Perhaps he was thinking about Ireland's peace-keeping role in the world. But perhaps he also had in mind the fact that the Army had never, until August 1969, even thought about the North in offensive terms. Again, no special knowledge is needed to know that such an offensive deployment to protect the minority was on the cards after the situation worsened in the North. For instance, an *Irish Independent* editorial warned in August 1969 against such a Northern deployment. Fr. Martin's remarks, along with Duggan's emphasis on the *internal* nature of military moves, seem to have the object of covering up what Irish military policy really was in 1969-70.

It is in the context of explaining army dispositions in the early 1980s that Duggan reveals: "Prior to 1969 there were no permanent military posts located north of a line from Gormanstown to Mullingar and Galway" (p281).

As for the context for Irish military planning: there is nothing so awesome as a society on the move—a rare phenomenon in the history of nations. Towards the end of 1968 the Catholic community in the North began to sense that 'Civil Rights' offered an avenue out of the stultifying situation, which Britain had imposed as the form of Partition, and began to move. And the more panic-stricken and violent the Unionist response was to street activity, the more the agitation gathered pace and weight. By August 1969 the movement of the Civil Rights juggernaut was irresistible. We saw Taoiseach Lynch commenting in early August to Britain's Ambassador Gilchrist on the *"Frankenstein monster"* which civil rights had become in the North (*1969: Ireland's Only Appeal To The UN* p10). Within days of saying that the Taoiseach himself had succumbed to Frankenstein's embrace, making a solemn television address which threatened Irish military intervention and maddened Unionists.

The seismic shift in the attitudes of a community which sensed the moment was right for an upward thrust carried all before it: dragged into the liberating avalanche were priests and people, mainstream politicians and revolutionaries.

In mid-August 1969 the Catholic community in the North broke through the carapace of non-intervention which the 26 County Government had generated in order to defend the degree of independence already won in the South. In emergency sessions the Irish Cabinet—at the urgent importuning of Northern elected and community leaders—agreed a new military policy towards the North as well as the terms of the speech which the Taoiseach made on 13th August.

One element of the new approach was to instruct the Army to prepare for incursions to protect Catholic life and property. The other was to facilitate the Northern minority in getting the weapons and training they needed to protect their out-numbered communities from those well-armed forces intent on maintaining Catholics in their traditional place.

That was the Government policy which was unilaterally overturned by Taoiseach Lynch when he succumbed to external pressure, changed tack and launched the Arms Conspiracy Trials.

Chapter Three

Help For The Northern Minority

"If Irish troops would not be sent in to the North, then they wanted guns"
Paddy Kennedy MP to
Hugh McCann, 16th August 1969

The Irish Government gave direct and indirect military assistance to the Northern Ireland minority from the 'Siege of Derry' of mid-August 1969 until Lynch's *volte face* of May 1970. This was quite apart from the instruction to the Army to prepare for incursions into Northern Ireland to protect lives and property; and to prepare to distribute weapons

Ways in which the Government helped were: public funds were allocated to subsidise the purchase of an armoury, and Captain Kelly was authorised to vet the weapons bought by the Central Citizens' Defence Committees and to bring them into Ireland; up to a dozen Intelligence Officers were deployed to liaise with the minority; money was allowed to be openly collected from the public for buying weapons; gun-running from Ireland to the North was permitted; some guns were allowed to leech from the Army to the minority; the Army trained civilians from the North; and a blind eye was turned to military training of Northern defenders organised by others. An unusual loan was raised on West German money markets by Finance Minister Haughey to provide for contingencies.

It might be added that it was not just Fianna Fail that gave military help to the minority. It also came from members of Fine Gael, the Labour movement, and republicans of all ways of thinking. People wanted to help because of the eloquent appeals from Northern leaders, and in response to news reports of what was going on.

"“protection” for the Catholic population"

Derry Nationalist fears of an imminent pogrom formed the lead story in the *Irish Independent*, the Fine Gael paper, on 11th August 1969, the day before the 'Siege' started. Eddie McAteer, the leader of the Nationalist Party, was quoted as saying:

> "“I believe and hope in this, our hour of trial, if we are to be beaten into the ground as a helpless and unarmed minority, I pray to God that our watching brethren will not stand aside any longer…”
>
> "Asked if he meant that the Irish Government should send troops across the Border in the event of trouble he said: “In any form”…" (Irish Independent 11.8.1969).

The 'Siege of Derry' was a turning point in the civil disorder in the North. Defence was organised more systematically, and community action became increasingly coherent. Catholic community confidence generated a leadership able to conduct negotiations with the States with which it had to deal.

A stream of individuals and delegations went South to canvass for practical support; while volunteers, practical help, and fact-finding delegations went North.

Northerners paid special attention to canvassing members of the Irish Government, and particularly the Taoiseach.

On Friday 15th August—two days after his 'idly by' speech—Lynch saw three delegations of public representatives, two from the Nationalist Party and one from Republican Labour. His file note says of Austin Curry MP, "the main spokesman" for the former, that he—

> "told me that the situation in towns such as Dungannon and Coal Island [sic] was explosive and especially urged me that any announcements I would make in relation to what we were doing should high-light the word "protection" for the Catholic population..." (NA 2000/6/658).

The following day, the Taoiseach's Department noted separate phone calls from Ivan Cooper MP and Paddy Kennedy MP. A file note says:

> "...Both said that the Catholic area of Ardoyne in Belfast was surrounded by Paisleyites and B specials and that the inhabitants were without any protection whatever. Unless British troops were moved in before night-fall, a massacre of the inhabitants of the area was inevitable. Shortly afterwards, the same information was conveyed to me by Mr. Brendan Halligan, General Secretary of the Labour Party in Dublin, who said that he had received the news from members of the Party - two Deputies and two Senators - who were on a fact-finding mission in Belfast. I immediately informed the Taoiseach..." (2000/6/658).

Paddy Kennedy MP came to Dublin that same night, along with two other Northern MPs, in an attempt to see the Taoiseach. A file note by Hugh McCann, Secretary of the Department of External Affairs, was sent both to the Taoiseach and to the Secretary to the Department of Justice, Peter Berry:

> "*Secret*
>
> *Visit of Northern Ireland M.P. to Department*
>
> ...
>
> 2. I reached the Department around 10.20 p.m. and saw the delegation in the waiting room. They were Mr. Paddy Devlin (N.I. Lab. - Belfast), Mr. Paddy O'Hanlon (Ind. - South Armagh) and Mr. Paddy Kennedy (Rep. Lab. - Central Belfast)... Mr. Kennedy, who was the main spokesman, said that the B Specials were on the loose in Belfast; that there was continuous sniping and that people were being shot down. More and more Catholics were being forced into the Falls Road area and were being forced further and further up in the Falls. Soon the whole Catholic population would be concentrated in this area and they would be

massacred. Bogside in Derry was mild compared to this. The Catholics there would have to defend themselves and their homes and they had to see the Taoiseach. They could not return to the North until they had seen him. If Irish troops would not be sent in to the North, then they wanted guns and they could not leave without definite answers to these questions. The situation of the Catholics in Belfast could not continue without protection. As regards guns, nothing need be done openly or politically - a few hundred rifles could easily be "lost" and would not be missed..."

McCann responded that—

"The request about troops or arms was a matter for Government and perhaps even for Dáil decision. I stressed that this did not indicate any lack of concern by the Government.

5. All three M.P.s reacted vehemently to this response saying that it was a fob off and an exasperating attitude. Mr. Devlin who was more angry and emotional than the others made for the door saying that he would see to it that he saw the Taoiseach before he left Dublin. He came back and muttered something abusive about the Government being responsible for deaths. All three then walked out of the Department led by Mr. Devlin. I followed them to the hall door and again expressed to Mr. Kennedy that they should not infer any lack of concern on the part of the Government or that such action as was open to them would not be taken...." (A handwritten note, possibly by Mr. O'Dowd, Mr. Lynch's Private Secretary, says he rang the police to strengthen the guard on Mr. Lynch's home, but that this had already been done; 2000/6/658).

This attempt to see the Taoiseach was reported in the *Irish Independent* (18.8.69), under the headline, *Policy Of Regime 'Similar To Hitler's'*. The MPs were reported as declaring that—:

""While aid to refugees from the Six Counties is welcome, the direst need at the moment is to get food clothing medical supplies and other appropriate material through to the beleaguered areas in Belfast, Derry and elsewhere. If this is not done immediately the loss of life will dramatically multiply."

The three M.P.s appealed to the Irish people and Government to help them, and implored the Government to make this aid available without delay, as delay could prove fatal.

"This is a cry of desperation. We make it in the full knowledge of the situation of the people we represent. We implore you not to abandon us in agony..." "

The demand for guns is not mentioned as such, but merely hinted at with the reference to *"other appropriate material"*.

In the second week of September 1969 Captain Kelly met Gerry Fitt MP, the leader of the Republican Labour Party, in Belfast. Fitt spoke in general terms (expounding the views of Pearse and Connolly), then the conversation became more focussed. Captain Kelly told Fitt—

"...all the people I had met right across from Derry to Belfast asked for arms to defend themselves and their communities. I suggested that at that stage, there might be a period of calm in which to organise and put a case to the Irish Government, saying something to the effect that governments are slow to move. Mr. Fitt responded with passion:

"You're wrong. You say we have time to work out something. I tell you we haven't. We're sitting on a tinder-box here. Violence could break out at any time, today or tomorrow, tonight, even tonight, it's not too late yet. It could happen any minute."

At that moment, the room door burst open and Mrs. Fitt stood there.

"It's on Gerry. It's on, Gerry", in a half-whispered shout.

"Where?"

"Round the corner, the New Lodge."

"What did I tell you? It's not next month we need arms. It's now, now, in the next five minutes maybe. Come on, come with me". Mr. Fitt led the way out.

He stopped in the hall to pick up a red phone. He rang Lisburn (British Army Headquarters in Northern Ireland) and demanded the immediate dispatch of soldiers to the scene. Outside, a couple of hundred yards away, two mobs faced each other down a narrow street. The RUC lined up in front of the Protestant mob while vigilantes, with linked arms, held back the Catholics. Stolidly accepting the occasional punch from the more fanatical of their co-religionists, the vigilantes successfully contained the heaving, screaming mob until the arrival of the British army. The soldiers took up position in front of the Catholics while an officer negotiated with their representatives. He handed a loudspeaker to Gerry Fitt, who did an excellent job in calming down the crowd. Finally, with police and military forming a dual security screen between the rival factions, passions cooled and confrontation was avoided for another night.

...the Fitt demand for immediate arms had been dramatically emphasised... I said I would head for Dublin the following morning and stress the urgent need for arms..." (*Thimble Riggers* p12).

Captain Kelly had his report typed by an Intelligence confidential typist and gave it to his chief: "As was usual with all my reports, Colonel Hefferon brought this report to the attention of the Minister for Defence" (ibid p13; Captain Kelly stayed with Paddy Kennedy, the Republican Labour MP, that night, see Kennedy press conference report, IT 9.5.70).

On Sunday, 28th September 1969, Northern leaders held a public meeting in Dublin to build support and collect money for guns. Sir Andrew Gilchrist, British Ambassador, in a *Confidential* telegram to London, reported that the crowd was:

"...addressed by Northern anti-Unionist leaders including Messrs. Ivan Cooper, Eammon McCann, Austin Currie, Paddy O'Hanlon, Paddy Kennedy, Aidan Corrigan, Finbarr O'Doherty and Miss Margaret Collins... O'Doherty told the crowd that the collection being taken from them would be used to buy machine guns and revolvers "so that we will not be unprepared when the Paisleyites attack us and burn us out of our homes"..." (FCO 33 759).

Apart from the open way in which money for guns was being collected in the South, what is of interest to us here is the very mixed platform from which it was being done.

The delegations from the North continued to besiege the Irish political establishment to beg for military help into April 1970.

In his speech from the dock during the Army Conspiracy Trial, John Kelly, the Citizens' Defence Committee leader, stressed that every social class and political tendency was united in this endeavour to get military help:

> "...these delegations were people from the Six Counties area, a collection of people of varying shades of minority political opinion...
>
> [the delegations]...contained people of all shades of political opinion within the Six Counties. They contained people like myself who were republicans, but they also contained people of no particular point of view... who were drawn together to organise the defence of the minority areas in what we felt then was a Doomsday situation.
>
> They provided first aid posts; they engaged in fire-fighting, prevention of looting, and liaison with the British Army. But their primary function was to organise the defence of the minority community. They were concerned with obtaining arms; they were concerned with vigilante duties; they were concerned with the manning of the barricades and the enforcement of discipline. They were, in effect, the administration of a very large part of Derry's Bogside and a very large part of Belfast...
>
> I myself accompanied the delegations which met the Taoiseach and Mr. Blaney, delegations which met Dr. Hillery and Mr. Haughey, delegations which met Mr. Gibbons and Mr. Lenihan...
>
> ...I want to be very emphatic that we were coming from all parts of the Six Counties... not to be entertained, but to elicit in so far as we could what was the opinion of this Government in relation to the Six Counties.
>
> We did not ask for blankets or feeding bottles. We asked for guns and no one from Taoiseach Lynch down refused that request or told us that this was contrary to Government policy..."

The one group which John Kelly did not mention was the Catholic Ex-Servicemen. These former personnel of the British armed forces were to the fore in organising defensive measures and played a very important role.

John Kelly went on to explain that, in a meeting with the Defence Minister on 3rd March 1970, "...we discussed very thoroughly with... Mr. Gibbons... the position in the Six Counties and the necessity for arms being provided against any breakdown in the society there". At around this time the Department of External Affairs was estimating that there was a 30 : 70 chance of such a breakdown happening.

Government Provisions

Up to a dozen Army Intelligence Officers were seconded to work with the Northern minority. The Taoiseach did not deny this deployment in a May Dail debate during the Arms Crisis.

Captain Kelly, however, had a special position amongst these officers.

At the end of August a civil rights information office was established in Monaghan town. *Private Eye* was not far off the mark when it said that it "is paid for by the Government out of secret service funds" (12.9.69). Intelligence Officers kept a regular liaison with Defence Committee activists through this office. That Autumn of 1969 the *United Irishman* named Captains Drohan and Duggan as being involved.

To finance help to Northerners the Cabinet agreed—

> "that a sum of money—the amount and the channel of disbursement of which would be determined by the Minister for Finance—should be made available from the Exchequer to provide aid for the victims of the current unrest in the Six Counties and... that machinery be established with the object of maintaining permanent liaison with opinion in the Six Counties" (NA 2000/6/658).

The following statement was issued by the Government after the Cabinet Meeting of 16th August:

> "*Northern Relief.*
> The Minister for Finance has announced that the Government is making available adequate funds for the relief of victims of the disturbances in the Six Counties. These funds will be administered mainly by the Irish Red Cross Society..." (NA D/T 2000/6/658).

Captain Kelly tells us:

> "I had learned through a contact in Belfast that, shortly afterwards, Mr. Haughey had promised £50,000 to a three-man Belfast delegation. This promise of money from the Dublin Government was announced at a gathering of Defence Committee people in Belfast in a matter of days. It was also stated at the meeting that the money was for the purchase of arms. I informed Mr Haughey of this development. He was very annoyed that the matter of the money should be bruited around in such an indiscreet way and instructed me to inform the Central Defence Committee that money would not be forthcoming from his department until a proper and reliable finance committee was formed. An eminently respectable committee was quickly put in place. Those operating and signing the cheques under the aegis of this committee were three of the more eminent men in the Northern Ireland Nationalist community. Mr. Haughey was quite happy with the new arrangement and moneys from the "aid fund" were paid into a bank account in Clones, County Monaghan. This was the birth of the Belfast Fund for the Relief of Distress, which was eventually allotted £70,000 or thereabouts by the Irish Department of Finance" (*Thimble Riggers* p31).

The three Northern Ireland trustees for the Relief Fund were two Stormont MPs Paddy Kennedy (Republican Labour), and Paddy Devlin (Northern Ireland Labour Party), along with Mr. Macrory.

Around 20th September 1969 Captain Kelly went to Derry and found that "the Nationalists there looked to the South for assistance" (p13). This time Kelly reported not just to Colonel Hefferon but to a member of the Cabinet directly. He saw—

> "Neil Blaney, who, I understood, was a member of the sub-committee appointed by the Cabinet to deal with Northern Ireland affairs. I had a general discussion with Mr Blaney who arranged that I should meet Charles Haughey, then Minister for Finance, another member of the sub-committee, that same evening. I covered the same ground with both Ministers, conveying to them the sense of urgency and the emphasis laid by the minority in the North, endorsed by Gerry Fitt, on the necessity of arms for defensive purposes. This did not take either Minister by surprise, because, since August, many deputations had come south seeking arms as a first priority, but what possibly did surprise them, as it had certainly surprised me was the virtual unanimity among a very representative cross-section of the Nationalist community that some type of defensive weaponry was necessary and should be made available" (*Thimble Riggers* p13-14).

Both Colonel Hefferon and Captain Kelly saw Haughey in his Kinsealy home in the last week of September (see testimony to Public Accounts Committee, Booklet No. 7 para 4102).

This was Captain Kelly's last visit to Northern Ireland; afterwards he met his contacts elsewhere. "It seems that the identity of other intelligence officers who had visited the Six Counties had come to the notice of the authorities there... Colonel Hefferon issued an order that in future no intelligence officer was to enter Northern Ireland without his specific permission—a permission which I had never any necessity to seek" (p13).

After this Captain Kelly met Mr. Blaney about once a week. They exchanged information, with Blaney able to contribute a lot to the "intelligence picture" (p14) because of his many contacts in the Northern Ireland. Captain Kelly assumed that Blaney "was reporting to the Cabinet as a whole". He was also keeping Hefferon informed of his contacts with the two Ministers.

Nationalist Politics

Captain Kelly met John Kelly for the first time in Gerry Fitt's house in Belfast on 13th September 1969. About a year later both were in the dock in Dublin.

John Kelly had been involved in the IRA 1956 campaign and served six years in prison. Afterwards he left active republicanism and rebuilt his life. He got a good job (site planning officer for ICI). He became a family man, and his interest turned to Labour issues. When the crisis came in Belfast, he was approached by the community to help organise defence, chiefly because of his military experience. He agreed reluctantly, knowing that return to activism would jeopardise the security he had known for a few years but, in view of the crisis, did not feel he could refuse. When he became an organiser for the Citizens' Defence Committees, he got drawn back into activist republicanism once more.

The self-rule activity organised by the CDCs had the effect of excluding the functions of the Stormont State. This created a situation of *"dual power"*—which was why Unionists were so angered by the establishment of 'no-go' areas behind the barricades.

(This capacity for autarchy shown by the Catholic community could have resulted in a new kind of political party, akin to developments in the Irish Republic during the War of Independence. Then the revolutionary movement attempted to oust British-organised services and replace them with the incipient forms of its own state organisation. While there was no prospect of excluding the Stormont State from Catholic areas in Northern Ireland, the development of a political party which took responsibility for its community would have had significant political results. One of these was that defence work would have been under civil control.

There can be little doubt that John Kelly would and should have been in the leadership of the new nationalist party that was in the making—an organisation which would encompass both a political and defence dimension—and which would have closely interacted with Irish Government. But the Arms Conspiracy Trials nipped that development in the bud. Instead of a community party, the SDLP came into being. Andrew Boyd was not much exaggerating when he wrote in the *New Statesman* on 28th August 1970 that the Party was "formed from the top and seems to have few, if any, roots in the general population", but the real complaint against the SDLP was that its focus was on parliamentary, rather than community, action.)

Weapons

During the first Arms Conspiracy Trial, the Judge clarified what the defence case was:

> "*Mr. Justice O'Keeffe* asked them to suppose for a moment that the plans made to deal with an impending danger were that arms should be imported by a channel other than the normal Army purchasing channel and that, when they arrived in Dublin, they would be taken over and put in Army magazines, which would clearly be a good defence if it could be established.
>
> *Mr. McKenna* [prosecution]: There would be no crime.
>
> *Mr. Justice O'Keeffe*: I take it that is the nature of the defence…
>
> *Mr. Finlay* [for Captain Kelly]: That is undoubtedly the nature of the defence. Any consignment of arms with which my client was concerned was to be brought into the control and possession of the defence forces and held here against the contingency of subsequent distribution…" (IT 26.9.1970).

The Defence was able to make the case that this was in fact what happened. The Director of Military Intelligence, a prosecution witness in the September trial, gave the following evidence:

> "*Mr. McKenna* [prosecution]: From what Captain Kelly said to you, who were these arms to be for?
> *Colonel Hefferon:* They were to be for the Northern defence committees, in the event that a situation would become necessary, in the event of the Government agreeing to them going to them…
> *Mr. Justice O'Keeffe*: What was going to happen to them in the meantime?
> *Colonel Hefferon:* I gathered that they were to be put in a safe place pending a decision…

The Army Intelligence chief went on to say that Captain Kelly

> "was acting as an officer who was a go-between for the defence [committees] and the Government…
> …From February 6th or so when this directive was issued which indicated a firmer attitude towards the planning, I had many conversations with Captain Kelly in which he kept me informed of delegations coming down from Northern Ireland that the Ministers may have met… they had been promised support… arms and ammunition and gas masks… in conversations with various Government Ministers they had been promised help in this matter…
> *Mr. Finlay* [for Captain Kelly]: Did you tell the Minister that Captain Kelly had gone abroad for the purpose of vetting arms [around February 16th]?
> *Colonel Hefferon:* I did.
> *Mr. Finlay*: Would I be correct in saying that Captain Kelly had suggested to you that arms should be met by ordinary Army personnel and stored in Cathal Brugha Barracks?
> *Colonel Hefferon:* He mentioned it to me at one stage and I thought it would be impossible. It would attract tremendous attention and once the arms were got into Army custody it might be difficult to get them out again.
> …when I say the Army I mean the Quarter-master General…" (IT 29.9.1070).

The main thrust of Colonel Hefferon's evidence was that the arms importation was an official operation. But that did not mean it could be treated in a normal Army way: he warned Captain Kelly against using regular Army facilities and personnel for handling these weapons as that would mean that secrecy could not be maintained. There was the further consideration that, if the weapons were treated like the Army's own ordnance, there would be difficulties in removing the large quantities in question for distribution in the North. It emerged at the Trials that Captain Kelly devised a plan for storing the weapons in the grounds of a Border monastery until the Government authorised distribution to begin.

Training

The Army trained Northerners formally and informally.

We know about one group that was formally trained. At the Arms Trials, Colonel Hefferon was asked by Niall McCarthy (Haughey defence) about a group of men trained at Dunree Camp—

"...was any training provided?... Who were the people being trained? *Colonel Hefferon:* They were the people of Derry..." (IT 29.9.1070).

Captain Kelly explains how the Irish Army came to train Northern civilians:

"In September [1969], a serious situation had arisen in Derry city. The local Unionists were putting pressure on the British army commander in the area to take drastic action to bring the Bogsiders to heel. Eventually, a leading Unionist threatened that if the army did not act, his constituents would take the law into their own hands, stating that if something was not done "the streets of the city would run red with blood". Word leaked through to the Bogside and a decision was taken to fight in the event of any such attempted pogrom. Little or no arms were available and, even if there were, there were no men trained to use them. Accordingly, three people sought a meeting with Colonel Murt Buckley of the Irish army in Letterkenny, Co Donegal. Their request was simple: urgent facilities for training men, and arms to be made available close to the border in Donegal.

Colonel Buckley was sympathetic to the plight of the Derry men, but was not inclined to meet such a request. He was bluntly asked to put the matter to higher authority. A week later, word came down that the training was to take place, with the first intake reporting to Fort Dunree, at the northern tip of Donegal overlooking Lough Swilly. The training, authorised by the Minister for Defence, was an intensive week's course in small arms, grenades and mortars, with a section of two, ten or twenty men, reporting each week over a period of several weeks. The men were to be drafted into An Forse Cosanta Aithiuil (FCA), the local territorial force, providing a Donegal address to meet with army regulations.

Nine men enrolled for the first week's training and were due to return to Derry on Friday, October 3. On that day, I was in the office of the Director of Intelligence in my capacity as Personal Staff Officer when word came through that the training at Fort Dunree, which was a secret and undercover operation, was likely to be the subject of newspaper comment over the weekend. The Director attempted to contact the Minister or the Chief of Staff, but when neither was available, he decided on his own initiative to postpone further training for the moment...

The only reason for the interruption of the planned training of a considerable number of Northern Ireland citizens in the use of arms was the fear of publicity and, in fact, at the time I got the strong impression that Colonel Hefferon's decision to intervene with the training was not received altogether with favour at a higher level..." (*Thimble Riggers* p15-16, There was a sequel to this story. During the Scarman Tribunal hearings, the Secretariat at the Department of Defence feared that the Dunree training might be mentioned by witnesses in their evidence. Captain Kelly was instructed to prevent this from happening and did so).

Private Eye featured the story of the training of the Derry people in its issue of 24th October 1969:

"Ever since the riots in Northern Ireland last August, a number of volunteers have taken the road from Derry to Letakenny (sic], across the Border, and thence to the FCA (territorial army) training grounds at Rockhill Camp and Dunree Camp. The men, many of whom are unemployed, were handpicked by members of the citizens defence committee in Derry. The men were taken to the two camps and put on a 'crash' course in the use of rifles and machine guns. They are then dispatched back to Derry with assurances that in the event of serious civil strife in the town, guns will be made available..." (p4; the report is on less sure ground when it goes on to speculate about the reasons for holding the courses, and the forces opposed to them).

I have been informed that the men in this first group were paid by the Irish Government for their attendance at this training course.

Training of Northerners continued on a discreet basis. Rather than bringing down groups, individuals were allowed to enlist in the FCA and in the regular army. Those joining the FCA had to give a Southern address, but this rule did not apply to those joining the permanent defence force.

The matter was raised in the Dail on 21st May 1970, after Lynch's *coup*, in the following manner:

> "Mr. Patrick Hogan (F.G., Tipperary South) asked the Minister for Defence if citizens of Northern Ireland were brought into the State anytime last year for special Army training, and Mr. Paddy Belton (F.G. Dublin N.E.) asked if civilians were afforded the training facilities of the F.C.A. in Donegal recently.
>
> Mr. Cronin [successor to Jim Gibbons] replied that the implication in the questions was that civilians had been given military training by the defence forces. There was nothing new in this allegation. Similar allegations had been made from time to time and it had always been made clear that military training in the State was given only to duly enlisted members of the defence forces.
>
> Persons resident in any part of Ireland were eligible for enlistment in the permanent defence force provided they were not ineligible on other grounds. "While under defence force regulations a person ordinarily resident outside the State is not, subject to certain exceptions, eligible for enlistment in the F.C.A., it has not been the practice of a testing officer to question the addresses within the State given by potential recruits as their place of ordinary residence." ...
>
> Dr. Hugh Byrne (F.G. Dublin N.W.) asked if the Minister would agree that it would be easy for people from outside the 26 Counties to enrol in the F.C.A. and get summer training: the drop-out rate of two-thirds per year lent weight to the suspicion that this in fact had been going on for some time..." (IT 22.5.70).

Defence Minister Cronin's replies were carefully phrased to imply that there was no truth in the *"allegation"* being brought forward by Fine Gael TDs.

That position was not sustainable, and it was abandoned in the Arms Conspiracy Trials. In the report below, Mr. Gibbons was being questioned by Mr. Finlay (counsel to Captain Kelly and later Chief Justice):

> *"Mr. Finlay* [regarding the FCA]: It is not intended for the purpose of training people outside the Republic?
>
> *Mr. Gibbons:* Not strictly speaking.
>
> *Mr. Finlay:* Do you agree that the enrolment of the people of Derry on your order into the F.C.A. was an unorthodox method of achieving of what you thought a proper objective?
>
> *Mr. Gibbons:* Yes.
>
> *Mr. Finlay:* It was making use of the defence forces to assist the minority in Derry to be in a position to defend themselves?

Mr. Gibbons: Yes.

Mr. Finlay: You thought that a proper action to be taken at that time?

Mr. Gibbons: Yes.

Mr. Finlay: You thought it a proper action to be taken at that time?

Mr. Gibbons: Yes, at that time of serious stress and strain.

Mr. Gibbons added that the nature of the training would have been determined by the Army but he would imagine that it would have application to the conditions in which the Bogsiders might find themselves, and he presumed that it would be elementary training in the use of weapons.

Mr. Finlay: Did you make any enquiries as to what guns they had when they went to Derry?

Mr. Gibbons: I am quite certain they had no weapons that were properly Irish Army weapons, or, for that matter, any weapons.

Mr. Finlay: Had you any information as to what guns were available to these people after they had been trained and sent back to Derry?

Mr. Gibbons: No.

Mr. Finlay: Did you give any consideration to this question?

Mr. Gibbons: From what I could gather and from what had previously happened in Derry up to that time, the paucity of guns in the area being defended was self-evident.

Mr. Finlay: They had practically no guns.

Mr. Gibbons: That would appear to be the case.

Mr. Finlay: Would you agree it was pointless to train the men in the use of guns unless they were going to get guns?

Mr. Gibbons: I would not agree.

Mr. Finlay: What was the point of training them in the use of guns if they were not going to get guns?

Mr. Gibbons: My chief motivation in this gesture would be to convey to them that their dire straits were perceived by us and were sympathised with by us..." (IT 10.10.1970)

Mr. Gibbons found himself in a tricky position as a result of this acute questioning. He had to admit that the Government provided military training to Northerners, though they had no guns, and then tried to deny that Government had any interest or involvement in the supply of guns they might use their hypothetical training on!

Unofficial Responses

In addition to training conducted by the armed forces, the Government connived at informal camps set up by a variety of groupings, including republicans, which provided comprehensive military training for defenders of the minority.

Conor Lynch informs me that in late 1969, at a republican training camp in Leitrim, the weapons available were Bazookas, Lee Enfield Rifles, Thompsons, Sten Guns, Bren Guns, a couple of machine guns and every form of pistol.

On 12th September 1969 *Private Eye* noted the changed approach to 'law and order':

> "...For the last few weeks there has been an unofficial amnesty for all manner of republican militants whose activities even a few months ago were sternly curtailed by the Eire police. Men who previously would have been clapped in jail if they appeared in combat jackets are moving freely about Dublin making contacts and plans as they have not done since 1921... Other organisations [that is, apart from the IRA], more efficient and better equipped, have attracted considerable support, and are openly fraternising with Army units on the Border."

The magazine later suggested that a Government decision was made in August 1969 that "the Border would be left open and no steps would be taken to stop the importing of arms into Northern Ireland by members of illegal organisations" (22.5.1970; it is hard to know how to treat *Private Eye* reports. With hindsight many of them appear to be remarkably accurate, though with there tends to be bias, and some details are awry. Readers have to make their own judgement about this source).

Further Shipments

Peter Berry in his 'Diaries' mentions two consignments of weapons that came in through Dublin Airport during February 1970, which were "facilitated by named members of the customs staff". One was labelled agricultural parts and the other machine parts. Both were consigned to legitimate companies, but when asked to collect shipments they had not ordered by the customs, the firms in question found that "the cargo... had disappeared". It seems,

> "...the "S Branch" were aware from a highly confidential source of the dates the cargos were cleared, the names of the accommodating customs and airport officials and of the individual members of the IRA involved but for fear of a leak-back which might disclose the source the importations were not reported-on in writing. They had no doubt of the authenticity of their information" (Vincent Browne's *Magill* June 1980 p58).

We do not know what was in those February cargos, nor whether the arms were for the IRA or the Citizens' Defence Committees: Mr. Berry does not care to make that distinction in his 'Diaries'.

Army Weapons For North

Lt. Col. Duggan made a curious remark about the Army weapons inventory in the extract quoted in the last Chapter. He said that, after August 1969, *"battalion organisations were constantly changing, causing confusion... in accounting for weapons and equipment..."* (*History*, p279). This suggests that the Army was not able to account for all its weapons after that crisis period. Col. Duggan attributes the shortfall in weapons, the amounts and nature of which he does not specify, to the disruption in commands caused by formation of the groups deployed to the Border. That might have provided a pretext to explain the shortfall in stocks, but does not account for it.

My information about Army practice suggests that it had a rigorous system of monitoring its arsenals, with casings having to be handed in for every bullet being fired in practice sessions.

We know that fearful Northern civilians approached Army posts along the Border after and asked for guns. It seems reasonable to conclude that these requests were granted, in some cases at least.

But it was not just along the Border that Army weapons 'migrated' to defenders of the Northern minority. I have been informed of an avenue of supply in the Cork area of the Army Southern Command.

A retired official of the Irish Transport and General Workers' Union told me a story which I found incredible. Michael Mullen, the General Secretary of the ITGWU, set up a Northern Relief Fund in August 1969 to which members of the Union were invited to pay 1/- a week. Some money from this fund, which was lodged in the Chase Manhattan Bank, was used to buy weapons for the North.

My informant was put in contact with a Reserve officer from the Cork command of the Army, who offered to sell him brand new machine guns. There were two consignments and the weapons were brought North. It seemed that a number of Army men were involved.

I was told that the weapons were passed on unused in their packing cases, along with boxes of ammunition.

I felt very sceptical when I first heard this story. I could not see how arms could simply go 'missing' from Army stores—particularly brand-new machine guns.

But my informant said he thought he could find the Army Reserve Officer of 35 years ago, who had been the contact man. Thus it was that on a chilly Autumn day in 2005 we headed off in the direction of a Munster town. We stopped at a farm which he recognised and—Lo and Behold—an elderly man came out to the car. He was the officer in question, and he spoke to us at the entrance to his farm, not wanting us to meet his family. We spent about half an hour there, talking.

I was introduced as researching a book on the Arms Crisis which would help to vindicate Captain Kelly, whose life, and that of his family, had been blighted by the false allegations brought against him by the Lynch Government.

We appealed to this officer to provide an Affidavit which would explain the circumstances of the secret Arms Sales. We explained that his evidence would confirm the general Government policy of supplying arms to the North. But he was adamant that he would not—not even to vindicate the reputation of an innocent fellow-officer. However it was clear that he was uncomfortable with his refusal to help.

He agreed that he had several times provided weapons to my informant, but absolutely refused to go public about it.

I described the documents which I was turning up and which showed the Irish Government had a policy of arming the Northern minority. He still demurred: he had a grown-up family and they had no idea of that particular role which he had played. Other former Army officers were also implicated.

We questioned this officer about how it was that substantial numbers of weapons could disappear from the Army inventory without being missed. We asked him whether there had been some kind of authorisation from above to sanction the sales, and to cover up the shortfall. But he was evasive and would not admit that senior officers had authorised the transactions.

The explanation he offered about how he could provide machine guns was that rifles and ammunition often went missing from Army stores, as they were sought after for hunting rabbits! I thought this was an unsatisfactory answer, but he would not go beyond it. And he pleaded not to be named.

All I can say about the encounter is that it confirmed in a dramatic way what I had been told about Army weapons going to the North.

It is not possible to go further than that. This man was clearly shaken up by this apparition from thirty-five years ago, come to haunt his respectable retirement, and it would not be right to name him at present.

Of one thing I am certain, if machine guns with ammunition were allowed to leech from the Army, in the knowledge that they were being sent to the North, that occurred with the connivance of the Army command. And the documents reproduced in Chapter Two explain why they allowed such informal transactions to happen. After all, the Directive of 6th February instructed the Army to supply weapons for the defence of the minority.

Traceability might not have been a problem as the weapons in question might have been imported covertly, which is to say, outside British oversight.

Treaty Provisions

It could be that the weapons that were being released in this surreptitious way were part of consignments secretly brought in by the Irish Government outside the terms of confidential military agreements with Britain. The 1922 'Treaty' laid down maximum strength for the Irish Defence Forces, a provision which has never been revoked. And there are persistent rumours of secret codicils relating to military matters in the 1938 Agreement, under which the British Government returned the naval facilities which it had reserved to itself in Southern Ireland under the 'Treaty'.

It certainly seems to be the case that Britain at that time took a close interest in what arms Ireland was importing.

It will be remembered that in Chapter One we saw the Quartermaster General stressing the need to diversify Irish supply of weaponry and to find alternative suppliers. *Private Eye* reported on 12th September 1969 that: "Two shiploads of arms, mostly 9 millimetre artillery shells and 7.65 ammunition, have been unloaded secretly at night at the Dublin docks".

I would find credible in general the following details carried by *Private Eye* magazine on 22nd May 1970, a few weeks after Lynch changed Government policy, indicating that the Irish Government had armed itself beyond the permitted limits:

> "...the British Government, despairing any firm action from Lynch [against Ministerial/Army action to prepare to defend Catholic areas], began to make their own moves. A new British Ambassador to Dublin, Mr John Peak [sic] , was appointed, who, on his appointment, informed Hillery that he desired to use the clause in the 1938 Agreement giving the British the right to visit Irish Military establishments.
>
> This move is reported to have caused consternation in Government circles as it would be very hard to disguise the fact that the Irish Army had in the past few months armed beyond the limit agreed in 1938. At the same time, Britain stepped up her Naval patrols to cover the whole coast of Ireland..." [The Ambassador in question was John Peck.]

I have heard rumours to the effect that excess Irish ordnance was dumped at sea after the British started making enquiries, but have no way of corroborating that.

British Concerns

The British authorities still had concerns about Irish military intentions with regard to Northern Ireland in the Spring of 1970. In the first publication in this series, *1969, Ireland's Only Appeal To The UN*, it was noted that Dr. Hillery refused to give Lord Chalfont an assurance in mid-August 1969 that Irish forces on the Border presented no threat to Northern Ireland.

On 2nd March 1970 British officials returned to the theme of Irish intentions. Kelvin White of the West European Department (Foreign and Commonwealth Office) went to Dublin and met S.G. Ronan and E. Gallagher of the Irish Department of External Affairs. Gallagher reports in a *Secret* 'Note':

> "Mr. White probed quite deeply on the question of what we would do if there were widespread disorder in the North. He presumed that we would go to the United Nations and that each side would utter speeches condemning the other, probably more in pain than in anger. On this we responded by saying that a real breakdown in the North, which we frankly thought to be unlikely, would have incalculable consequences to which the United Nations might not be a sufficient answer and that it was up to the British to make sure that such a case did not arise. He enquired as to what we would do if, say, an Irish Battalion commander on his own initiative crossed the border, and again we replied by pointing out that there was no reason why this should happen. It could only be justified in a most extreme

case, say, a pogrom continuing for 48 hours in perhaps Armagh or Newry during which the British Army made no effort to protect the minority. We did not anticipate that such a situation could arise. Mr. White indicated that the British Army are in a position to be anywhere in force in the North in 90 minutes. There seemed to be a suggestion that in the course of this questioning by Mr. White that the British felt that in some unspecified circumstances we might create an international incident by crossing the border. On this we hinted that conditions had almost been ripe for such a thing in August if we had wanted an excuse; we had not done it then so that it was quite unnecessary even to think that we might look for such an excuse in the future. He finally seemed satisfied with this answer" (NA 2001.6.513).

The idea behind Kelvin White's assurance to the Irish about the British capacity to maintain order in the North seems to be that troops could control any disorder by their mere presence, but that was not borne out when they were first deployed to Belfast. Lack of numbers meant that they had to simply look on while Catholic homes were burned down and people driven out of interface areas. The numbers deployed in Northern Ireland at that time were not sufficient to give full protection in the event of multiple outbreaks of trouble.

One of the questions which Kelvin White put to the Dept. of External Affairs officials was, what if a Battalion Commander went on a rescue mission into the North of his own accord? It seems a curious question to ask. Did he have a basis for such a question?

It was just four days after this British/Irish encounter that an Irish Government official, "H.R.", happened to meet Ivan Cooper and prepared the report of their conversation, part of which was quoted in the last Chapter. Cooper was not optimistic about British ability to defend the minority:

"He agreed with my suggestion that the minority fears of violence, especially in rural areas, during this year, were well founded. When I suggested to him that a realistic assessment of another outbreak might be 70:30 against he said that in his opinion he would put the possibility much closer to even money than that. He maintained that the British troops might be able to contain situations in Belfast and Derry but he did not think that they could possibly control the rural areas. I said that my opinion was that the British could have sufficient troops anywhere in the Six Counties within twenty-four hours. He said that would be no good as all the damage could be done in the first six hours. The problem was how many lives would be lost before the troops could arrive in a rural area" (6.3.1970; NA 2001/6/5, 13).

In view of such reports, it was not surprising that the Government considered it necessary to assist the minority with self-defence.

Irish Army

The Army was ordered to train civilians engaged in defending the minority in the North.

Guns leeched from the Army to Northern defenders, probably on authority from above.

And the normal legal process was suspended to permit money to be openly collected from the public to buy weapons for the North; to permit the running of guns; and to allow training camps to be established.

The Army was at the centre of the Irish Government's military response to the Northern crisis for nearly a year. As the *Donegal Democrat* wrote on 28th August 1969, Ireland was "in arms as never before".

Private Eye reported on 12th September 1969 that: "A forward artillery unit has travelled to Derry to recconoitre [sic], and the army intelligence corps has not been inactive in the Border towns of Northern Ireland". This is credible: how else could the Army produce assessments of what it was possible to do?

Charles Haughey raised a Deutschmark loan on the West German money markets to provide for contingencies. *Private Eye* commented:

> "Militant officers in the army... were reported to be 'delighted' that the Irish Government now had spare cash in hand to cope with a military emergency" (ibid).

The period from August 1969 to May 1970 was a happy time for the Irish Army. Years of neglect and lack of purpose were wiped out and a new morale permeated the ranks. For the first time since the 'Emergency' during the Second World War, there was a real job of work to be done.

Here is the Army Press Office account of Army activity on foot of the Northern troubles 1969, which is called *The Year Of The North*. The title, significantly, has overtones recalling a book about the French invasion of Ireland during the 1798 Rebellion, *The Year Of The French*.

The report makes it clear that Army mobilisation, which started in August 1969, was escalated in November by the partial deployment of the FCÁ, and implies that readiness continues in February 1970. It starts by recalling the context for these moves, then quotes and summarises Taoiseach Lynch's television speech of 13th August:

> "And so we come to the 13th August. The following are excerpts from the account of the affair issued by our Government Information Bureau.
>
> "In spite of ample evidence of increasing tension (increasing polarisation of the two social groups in cities and towns in the North; riots in Belfast on August 3 leaving at least 80 people injured; Catholic families forced to leave their homes) and in spite of additional urgent appeals made to the Stormont Cabinet by the civil rights, political and other minority leaders, the Apprentice Boys' Parade took place in Derry on August 12 with Unionist M.P.'s participating.
>
> "As had been forewarned, trouble broke out and a major attempt at violent repression of the people of Derry by the police continued for 50 hours with a complete breakdown of law and order, large numbers of civilians and police being injured. For the first time ever in Britain or Ireland the police used tear-gas in riot control."

Taoiseach's Statement

On the evening of August 13 the Taoiseach, Mr. John Lynch, spoke to the nation on radio and television on the situation in the North. He pointed out that the Irish people had expressed their concern at the tragic events in Derry and elsewhere in the North. This concern was heightened by the replacement of the spirit of reform and inter-communal co-operation by the forces of sectarianism and prejudice.

Over several months past the Government had been patient and restrained, care had been taken not to exacerbate the position and their views had been made known to the British Government. However, the present situation could not be allowed to continue. The Stormont Government evidently was no longer in control of a situation which was the inevitable outcome of policies pursued by them for decades. The Royal Ulster Constabulary was no longer accepted as an impartial police force and the employment of British troops was unacceptable and not likely to restore peaceful conditions—certainly not in the long term.

The Government of Ireland could no longer stand by and see innocent people injured and perhaps worse. They had now, he said, requested the British Government to apply immediately to the United Nations for urgent despatch of a peace-keeping force to the Six Counties; the Irish Permanent Representative to the United Nations had been instructed to inform the Secretary-General of this request. The British Government had also been asked to see that police attacks on the people of Derry ceased immediately.

Since many of those injured did not wish to be treated in Six County hospitals Mr. Lynch announced that the Irish army authorities had been instructed to establish field hospitals in Donegal and other points along the Border where necessary.

Recognising that reunification of Ireland provided the only permanent solution of the problem, he announced that the Government intended to request the British Government to enter into early negotiations to review the present constitutional position of the Six Counties.

"All men and women of goodwill will hope and pray that the present deplorable and distressing situation will not further deteriorate but that it will soon be ended firstly by the granting of full equality of citizenship to every man and woman in the Six County area regardless of class, creed or political persuasion and, eventually, by the restoration of the historic unity of our country," said Mr. Lynch."

The report then passes lightly over any sensitive matters. Though the Army may not have been privy to secret Cabinet military policy, soldiers could hardly have missed the fact that the deployments were on a far different scale than that suggested by the cover story, defending Refugee Camps and Field Hospitals. The Army Press Office continues:

"It is not, of course, possible here and now to describe the military movements which followed on the decision of an Taoiseach. In any case, few readers of *An Cosantoir* are in need of any reminder of the way in which the routines of their own personal and domestic life were affected. Let us hope it can be said of each one of us that he did his duty and did it ungrudgingly, efficiently and to the full, in the best traditions of the Irish professional soldier...

Gormanstown Camp, for a variety of reasons, became the focal point of the world's interest in Ireland at this time. The Camp's location was a big factor.

Journalists found it quick and easy to reach either from Dublin or from Belfast and, of course, it did have the biggest number of refugees.... The refugees rose in number to a total of 651 (in three camps) on the 25th August. They then began to fall. There were, for instance, only 382 on 6th September but on the 9th another rapid rise set in and the figure 590 was reached on the 14th. They dropped (and stayed) below 500 on the 19th, below 400 on 9th October, below 300 on 21st October, below 200 on 6th November and are at time of writing under 100 (and, of course, in one Camp). The total casualties treated in the Field Hospitals came to 68, being 49 in the North Western Area and 19 in the area administered from Collins Barracks, Dublin.

We can recall the part played by the First Line Reserve by quoting An Taoiseach. "The Government," he said, "have decided to authorise the mobilisation of the First Line Reserve of the Defence Force so as to ensure that they will be in readiness for participation in peacekeeping missions". The final total of Reservists who reported was never published but the number was sufficient to put our under-strength regular units in a position to cope with the situation. The services rendered by the Reservists were valuable and deeply appreciated. An Fórsa Cosanta Áitiúil [FCA] had to wait a little longer for its turn but large numbers of its personnel were ready, willing and rarin' to go and they made (and are continuing to make) a whole-hearted and effective contribution to the security requirements of the situation when the time came

...

...[November 1969:] Our Rangers were in the forefront of the news by this time ("Fianóglaigh" is in many ways an admirable term and of highly respectable etymology but one suspects it may fail to achieve colloquial usage). In any case on 14th November they were demonstrating their vigorous skills in the Curragh to an assembled party of newsmen who were sufficiently impressed to wax enthusiastic in print the following day...

The dry language of an official communique marked an exciting turn of events for the FCÁ when, on 7th November, it was announced that, "To assist the Army in carrying out security duties, especially selected members of the FCÁ will be asked to undertake brief tours of military duty, e.g., at weekends, in their own localities as may be considered appropriate by the military authorities". We may anticipate events somewhat by mentioning here an official report just before Christmas by the Director of Plans and Operations to the Chief of Staff. It described in glowing terms the value of the services rendered to date by the FCÁ, saying "All Staff officers who have had occasion to inspect the outposts have been unanimous in their praise for the volunteers of the FCÁ, who are sharing the duties", and plenty more in the same strain.

...

L.E. *Macha* was withdrawn from service for routine boiler cleaning on 5th December. Her fishery protective duties were assumed by the research vessel belonging to the Department of Agriculture and Fisheries, *Cú Feasa*, and quite a furore followed as some sections of the news media seemed to entertain doubts as to the efficacy of this arrangement, and indeed even as to the general quality of our national arrangements for naval defence.

...

Christmas Eve saw the Chief of Staff boarding a helicopter to visit posts along the Border bringing seasonal messages of goodwill to those on duty there...

In his address to the troops... [he said:]

"...every regular soldier will be glad to join with me in acknowledging with

> deep gratitude the tremendous help and support we have got from our two Reserve Forces, The First Line Reserve and the FCÁ,. We could not do the job without them. The First Line Reserve has merged into our units on fulltime service, giving us that blend of civilian experience and military training which is so valuable.
>
> "As for the FCÁ... They are alert, intelligent, keen and correctly inquisitive, fully trustworthy to share any duty..."
>
> The Chief of Staff concluded by wishing the joys of the festive season and peace and happiness in 1970 to all ranks. He reiterated the appreciation of the Government, General Staff and other members of the Defence Forces of the vital work being carried out in the Border area and at vital installations.
>
> This is perhaps the best note on which to bring our review to a close, although there were a couple of loud and violent bangs left in 1969 at that stage...
>
> It would be a brave man who would venture into prophecy about what 1970 may bring... One way or another, we will "soldier on" (*An Cosantóir* Feb. 1970).

How ironic is that final paragraph! The last thing the author would have expected was that, within seven months, an Army officer would be facing criminal conspiracy charges for following Government orders.

The *"loud bangs"* referred to may refer to the explosion at Malvern Street public house on 22nd December (where a Catholic barman had been shot in 1966) and an explosion which damaged the O'Connell monument in Dublin on 26th December 1969.

The reference to the *Rangers/Fianóglaigh* may be noted. The work of this force in the crisis of 1969 seems to have been deliberately obscured since then. Col. Duggan does not list them in the Index to his *History*, while the *Defence Forces Handbook* for 1987 says the Army Ranger Wing was founded in 1980. It refers to Rangers existing before that, but makes no link with 1969.

Here is how *Private Eye* described the 1969 deployments of the Army on 22nd May 1970 (a few weeks after Lynch's *coup*):

> "The cream of the officers of the Army were sent into the North to organise the defence of the nationalist areas. These officers included the Irish experts on irregular warfare.
>
> Special units of the Army were to be set up called "Rangers" and composed mainly of Northerners..."

A review of *An Cosantóir* for 1969-72 shows the upbeat atmosphere had dissipated by the end of 1970. In 1969 the usual Christmas message to the troops had been augmented by a message from the Minister for Defence. Christmas 1970 saw no Christmas messages at all. And no review of Army activities appeared for 1970.

The content of the magazine becomes thinner after April 1970 for a couple of years, with some change in focus. At the turn of 1969/1970, a couple of articles examined the role of the FCÁ. And in January 1970 a piece seemed to have direct relevance to the role the Defence Forces, and/or possible irregular allies, might be asked to play, as set out by the Planning Board On Northern Ireland Operations (Documents 8-10). It was entitled, *The Mortar In Irregular Warfare*, and was a translation of an article by Captain Pedro Garcia Zaragoza of Spain, who noted:

> "Technically the mortar is a weapon of the utmost simplicity ...an ideal weapon to strike against objectives located in the middle of built-up areas... [etc, etc]
>
> The confluence of the foregoing characteristics leads us to a study of some tactical possibilities which, in irregular warfare (the main characteristics of which are speed, surprise, mobility and daring), make the mortar an indispensible [sic] weapon..." (*An Cosantóir* Jan. 1970).

It will be recalled that the use of mortars featured as part of the special training given to the Derry men (mentioned above).

When Taoiseach Lynch engineered the Arms Crisis the Army was back in limbo, if not worse. *Private Eye* reported that—

> "the purge of "dissident elements" in the Army (consistently denied by Government sources) proceeds apace.
>
> A tiny item in the *Irish Times* of 10th June reported that the commission of Capt F Drohan was to be "relinquished". Capt Drohan was described as "of the Air Corps", a modest epitaph for a man who was in fact the Air Corps Senior Intelligence Officer. The Command of the Irish army in the border areas is also regarded with some suspicion in Dublin, and Col T. MacDonald a hard-line loyalist has recently visited the area with a view to taking over command there. The recent "comb out" of "subversives" in Donegal had to be assisted by police from Dublin, Tipperary and other towns more than 250 miles away, due to the reluctance of some army units to take part." (19.6.1970; an earlier report, on 22nd May 1970, had the Army purge starting in January 1970. It will be recalled that Captain Drohan was one of the Intelligence Officers named by the *United Irishman* the previous Autumn, but I am not able to confirm that his leaving the Army had any connection with Northern duties.)

Another *Private Eye* report suggested that on 20th April 1970—

> "11 Army officers, including Paddy "Jock" Haughey, the brother of Charlie Haughey, were arrested and taken to Dublin Castle...
>
> The army officers, with one exception, refused to make any statements when interrogated by members of the MWO section of the Special Branch.
>
> Following these arrests, army officers who had been involved in intelligence work in Ulster assembled in Columb Barracks, Mullingar. When members of the Special Branch attempted to enter this Barracks to interrogate officers, they were shown the business end of a sub-machine gun and told in no uncertain terms to go away.
>
> When this was reported to Lynch he called in the Chief of Staff of the Army whom he had earlier consulted about the allegiance of the Army. At this meeting it was reported that a senior GHQ officer told Lynch that if the arrests and

interrogations of army officers was continued it would impose “an intolerable strain” on the allegiance of army officers. This is believed to be a reference to the red-alert standby that night of all units of the 6th Brigade.

It is believed that only a phone call from one of the dismissed ministers stopped this unit from visiting Dublin to have words with the Special Branch units who arrested the army officers…

…on 30th April, the British army mounted operation “Mulberry”. Ostensibly this was to be a search of the border counties for arms. But it was interpreted by the Irish General Staff as the first stage of an operation to help disarm the Irish army. Lynch was informed by the Irish General Staff who insisted that Lynch take action one way or another to clarify his position." (22.5.1970; the report goes on to suggest that the British Ambassador, working with Peter Berry—the mandarin running the Justice Department—then pressured the Taoiseach to take action against Cabinet Ministers, using Opposition Leader Liam Cosgrave as an instrument; I don't know what the 'MWO' section of Special Branch was, but it appears from the Trial that a section of this force answered directly to Peter Berry).

Again, I cannot vouch to the accuracy of this story, which is of a kind with others which have circulated informally since the Arms Conspiracy Crisis. It seems to suggest that Jock Haughey was an Army officer but that was not so..

The dismissed Minister who prevented the officers moving on Dublin is rumoured to be Charles Haughey. All I can say about this story is that I do not find it incredible. I first heard it from a source far removed from *Private Eye.*

Conclusion

Various ways in which the Irish Government facilitated the self-defence of Catholics in the North have been set out.

There was the allocation of public money, with signatories for the Northern Ireland Relief Fund including MPs who had been the most active in seeking guns. And the Government facilitated military training for Northern civilians.

Delegations to Dublin were given a sympathetic hearing and positive response.

Intelligence Officers were deployed to the North, including Captain Kelly.

Captain Kelly was authorised to vet weapons and arrange for their importation: as we have seen, Minister Gibbons did not deny in Court knowing in advance of his journeys to the Continent as part of his duties.

Afterword

Breaking the taboo on military adventures in the North by deploying troops to the Border in mid-August 1969 was a dramatic gesture of support for the Nationalist minority in the North by the Irish Government. But it was more than a gesture, the move reflected the new offensive military strategy which was being urged on the Army.

In his television speech of 13th August Jack Lynch implicitly threatened not to stand by if there were further serious attacks on Catholic areas.

As we have seen, those public military moves were more than matched by the private orders given to the armed forces: to plan for cross-Border operations; to liaise with the Defence Committees; to arm the minority; to train Northern civilians.

The liaison activities of Captain Kelly of Military Intelligence were part of this strategy. He often escorted Northern delegations coming to meet Irish Ministers, and he was authorised to assist with arms importation for the minority.

Up to eleven other Intelligence Officers were allocated liaison duties at the same time.

All of this was kept secret from the Irish public. When substantial troop movements—even of artillery units—belied the cover story of establishing field hospitals and refugee camps along the Border with Northern Ireland, the Taoiseaach and all Government agencies continued to deny any further purpose to the deployments.

And, indeed, no other military objectives seemed to have been agreed upon by the Cabinet—beyond a readiness to intervene militarily in the North, should circumstances warrant it. The implicit message was: there was not going to be another 'Siege of Derry', not in Derry nor anywhere else.

But even the mere decision to be ready to intervene had far-reaching implications. The Army had to be upgraded and embrace a new culture.

And the policy implied a more demanding and vigorous stance with regard to the way that Britain governed Northern Ireland. Up to that point, Britain had simply brushed aside Irish protestations about the governing arrangements of Northern Ireland. As we saw in the Introduction, it took that approach even when Dr. Hillery flew to London on a mission to warn Britain that the Apprentice Boys' march of 12th August constituted a serious flash point for instability. Foreign Secretary Michael Stewart simply declared that it was none of Ireland's business. The Cabinet decisions of August 1969 broke that rejectionist approach.

The appeal to the United Nations, Army mobilisation, and helping Northern Nationalists to arm themselves—these practical moves made Britain understand that it could not simply brush aside Irish Governments, that they had to be managed with some care. Unfortunately, the collapse of Dr. Hillery's morale after the UN adventure meant that Irish Governments could be handled fairly easily: as Oliver Wright said in November 1969, *"I am sure the Irish Government will be satisfied with very modest conversations on the subject with us" (Introduction)*.

Nevertheless, as we have seen, Irish military policy remained active, even after Wright's cynical assessment, for some months more. In fact, military preparations went up a gear in February 1970 with the formal Government Directive to the Army to prepare for Northern incursions and to arm the minority.

It was not until the Taoiseach changed his position in late April 1970, and took steps to stun public opinion in Ireland, that Wright's prediction of what the Irish would be satisfied with were to be fully realised.

It must be remembered that Britain did not find it expedient to give Ireland an input into Northern Ireland governance until the Provisional movement had come into being and started fighting for constitutional change with popular support. Involvement of the Irish Government was intended to re-establish its hegemony amongst Northern Catholics and to wean them away from their home-grown community political expression.

*

As a result of the civil rights movement Northern Ireland Nationalists ceased to be a passive adjunct of Southern political life, and began to find their own political expression. They began to act cohesively as a political force in their own right, looking after their own interests. In August 1969 Northern Nationalists had turned to Irish Governments for protection, but in doing so they displayed a new self-reliance and self-confidence, qute different to anything that had existed since Partition.

It seemed that a Northern movement was going to develop that would look after its own interests in partnership with Irish Governments. And that Northern naissance touched a responsive chord in the South. For some months it seemed that this was going to happen.

By initiating that Arms Crisis, Taoiseach Lynch punctured that development. Southerners largely relapsed into the old hands-off frame of mind towards the North. But the consequences in the North were momentous.

If Lynch calculated that the Northern Catholic community would simply settle down into the old pattern of acting as a cowed minority, looking southwards for instruction, he was much mistaken. One element, to become the SDLP, certainly came to tend in that direction. But the striking thing that happened was the creation of a new self-expression of Northern Nationalism, the Provisional Republican movement. There can be little doubt that this would not have taken off, but for the shock of Jack Lynch's Conspiracy prosecutions.

*

What launched the coming of age of Northern Nationalism was winning the 'Siege of Derry': that was the turning point in Catholic self-emancipation in the North.

The citizens of the Bogside made preparations to defend their area, expecting violent police incursions during the Apprentice Boys' march. And they fought the RUC to exhaustion. Reinforcements were needed. There can be little doubt that the military mobilisation announced in Jack Lynch's television speech of 13th September, was a factor in the Stormont decision not to deploy the B-Special paramilitaries and to request British aid instead.. On 14th August the armed Specials could be seen standing by ready for deployment. If they had been sent in, there surely must have been war. *Ad hoc* groups of Irishmen were already gathering at the Border, in response to the pleas of the Derrymen for outside help. Things would have escalated from there.

The Northern Ireland Government had to make the choice of either calling in the Specials to put down the Derry men, or of calling in the British Army (and ceding security power to Wetminster, temporarily as it was thought). I am sure that the Irish mobilisation, popular and military, helped to decide Stormont not to risk sending in the Specials. The Irish Government had been protesting against the force for some months. But it might be that Premier Chichester Clark did not realise, when he asked for British help, that the soldiers were not going to join the police in knocking down the barricades around the Bogside, but were simply going to send the police out of sight. I doubt if he would have asked for British help if he had realised that it was going to mean a victory for the Bogsiders.

The way the British Government treated the Northern Ireland administration after it could no longer maintain order came as a severe shock to Unionism, which believed that Stormont had virtual 'Dominion Status'.

However, Britain was thereafter careful not to hasten into constitutional change, even though it knew that it was badly needed—which is why Catholic alienation continued to develop and grow.

*

The military documents reproduced here show beyond doubt that Taoiseach Lynch was not simply a figurehead in the Irish Government in 1969-70. He was fully involved in military planning for the North—including the decision to facilitate the arming of the Northern minority. And his Parliamentary Secretary, Desmond O'Malley, was also Parliamentary Secretary to the Department of Defence. It was O'Malley that Lynch chose to succeed Micheal O Morain as Minister for Justice, after the abrupt change of direction of late April/early May 1970. In that position, O'Malley (a solicitor) was involved in preparations for the Arms Conspiracy Trials.

The documents reproduced in this book show that the Arms Conspiracy prosecutions were quite unwarranted.

That was the verdict of the Court too, but it was to be a limited victory. On the individual level, the defendants in the Arms Conspiracy cases were left with their lives in a shambles. They had their victory in court, only to have it filched away from them by manipulation of public opinion. There was never any redress in the form of an akcnowledgement that the prosecutions were unwarranted. Their reputation was tainted in the new *Fine Fail* atmosphere.

These documents falsify much of modern commentary on the Arms Crisis, which is predicated on the idea that the Taoiseach was either kept in ignorance, or was manipulated by others.

But the question remains: why did Lynch change course, and what decided him on the further step of criminalising some of those who had been actively involved in the military policy of his Government, and not others. What did he hope to achieve with the Show Trials of September-October 1970? Those questions remain for the next publication in this series, which will examine the Conspiracy Trials and associated events.

But it is incontrovertible that the psycho-drama of those months, April to October 1970, had a profound effect on public opinion, both in the North and the South—but in different ways. A fissure was created in Fianna Fail and in the heart of Irish society. The Catholics of the North were thrown on their own resources: they had been made to understand that any change in their position would be won by their own efforts.

Appendix

Comments On Chapters One And Two

[A retired Army Officer has provided the following comments:]

It is obvious that the Government knew, from early on, that it might be forced to intervene, militarily, in the Six Counties, if matters deteriorated there—if, for instance, pogroms against the minority occurred and British Army forces stood aside. It is also obvious that the military might be utilised in such a situation, especially where civilian lives were at risk.

There is an amazing Army admission that it never considered plans for an invasion of the North, as no Government ever intimated other than "unity by consent". But an army doesn't know what Government will be in power, to-morrow; what any Government's policy will be to-morrow; what they, the military, will be asked by Government to implement, to-morrow. Therefore, the military must be ready at any time, to inform the Government of the day what it can do in this situation and what it can't do in this other situation. It is not up to the military to decide, or interpret, what a Government may or may not do; rather it is the military's job to tell the Government what it, the military can or cannot do, depending upon what the Government might ask it to do, especially in a changing, fraught situation; especially when the North was there, for years, a festering sore and one which might erupt at any time with dire consequences. For some time, prior to 1970, there had been a build-up. Matters were deteriorating in the North. Things were bound to come to a head. As they did.

Meanwhile, in the Republic, the Army was in a state of neglect. Equipment was antiquated. Transport was inadequate. There were no APC's [Armoured Personnel Carriers]. Armoured fighting vehicles were at a premium. The RCP (Relative Combat Power) *vis-a-vis* British forces, in the North (and their re-inforcement capability) was heavily in Britain's favour. Air supremacy would also lie with Britain. The state of the army was a frightful reflection upon the Government and upon the Army chiefs. (While the army must be subordinate to the Government, there comes a time for the grand gesture—and it had come and passed—wherein some Army Chief would say 'Enough! This is wrong. I cannot go along with it. The country is being undersold. I resign'. But this never happened. Things pottered along. The North seethed. The South stood by. Until the eruption. Then the Government sat up. It had to do something—or appear to. Circumstances might force its hand. The omens were bad. Send for the 'cavalry'.)

The First Step mobilisation plans (page 86) show the army inadequacies. The RCP is frightening. The measures to re-inforce are pathetic. Why the unit in Cyprus was not repatriated is a mystery. The pussy-footing that ensued between the Government and the military is shameful. The analysis by the military is poor. It had a capability, but this was, it seems, overlooked.

The army could have taken West Derry with a quick, battalion size, thrust from Donegal. The River Foyle would supply it with a natural barrier. It would take the Bridges and blow them. It would isolate and take any any British security forces positions in West Derry. Meanwhile, it would arm Citizens' Defence members in Derry. Small incursions along the border would similarly arm minority groups, but the principle of Concentration of Force (Derry)—especially where there are military inadequacies—would have been achieved. The ball is now in the British court. The Creggan Heights and the Bogside—with the Foyle and its destroyed bridges as a barrier—would provide strong-points. What would the British do? There would be intense Government to Government interaction; diplomats would be in overdrive; the situation would be internationalised, the UN would be involved. General McEoin's 24 hour occupation of Newry palls in comparison. He was no Rommel, but here he deliberately misled.

Would the British mount all out attack? Would their Government permit such? Or forbid it? Would there be an Army mutiny? The Irish Army would run a rescue corridor back into Donegal. The Irish Government would announce its intentions were merely benevolent; it would be willing to co-operate with the British Army; it would conduct joint rescue operations. It would, by now, have sown the seeds of possible Anglo/Irish Government co-operation over the occupied territories. (Meanwhile the Border towns in the Republic would be blocked off by G.S. [Garda Siochana] from incursions from the North). For the first time since partition an Irish Government would be seen to have taken a positive step regarding its exiled citizens. Their morale, in turn, would rise. There would be casualties, inevitably and unavoidably—as there were, anyway, in subsequent years. But things would never be the same again! Derry was the key—not Newry. This should have been apparent to any trained military mind. It was the correct mission. It was achievable. It would put Britain on the back foot. The final outcome?—no one knows, for sure, but an improvement upon what actually ensued, is the least one would expect. This catalyst might have proven politically unstoppable. Though an all-out British attack would succeed in retaking Derry, it would take time; it would allow for world opinion, including Irish American interventions and UN initiatives to impose and influence. That all-out attack might never have occurred. The future would have differed.

Meanwhile, in the absence of this positive action, things returned to their normal abnormality. Capt. Kelly and others were sacrificed. Lives were unfairly adversely affected. Self-servers prospered. But, amazingly, Taoiseach Lynch, months later, when the hare had settled, is still discussing "incursions" with the Army. But, of course, "only if". But was it not always "only if"? Except that it was decided the "if" had arrived.

Index

For a list of publications
distributed by
Athol Books,
and much else,
visit

www.atholbooks.org